A+ Educators

A World-Class Tribute to Our Best Teachers

Randy Howe

The Lyons Press
Guilford, Connecticut
An imprint of The Globe Pequot Press

This book is dedicated to Caroline Griffin, Kirk Kehrley,
Cheryl Slaiciunas, and the rest of the Student Services team at
The Sound School.

The Lyons Press is an imprint of The Globe Pequot Press.

Text designed by Sheryl P. Kober

Library of Congress Cataloging-in-Publication Data is available on file.

ISBN 978-1-59921-565-5

Printed in the United States of America

10 9 8 7 6 5 4 3 2 1

Contents

Acknowledgments

I must acknowledge Holly Rubino for her A+ guidance and Alicia Solis for being at my beck and call whenever I needed feedback. And, of course, almost forgotten in a sea of anonymity by an unappreciative student who can't even take the time to name them by name, are all of the wonderful teachers I must acknowledge from MKES (Mt. Kisco Elementary School), Fox Lane Middle School, and Fox Lane High School.

Introduction

Every accomplished professional, no matter the field, has at least one person to credit as a mentor. This is a person who, early on, provided a pat on the back after a job well done and constructive criticism after the expected mistakes. A mentor's advice and feedback hold such sway that they might determine just how successful a person's future in the profession will be. In the case of a new teacher, mentors give feedback on lesson plans and classroom management; hints on how to balance school life, family life, and the continuing education requirements of certification; and help in navigating the tricky waters of special education—just to name a few key areas of influence. As the new teacher gains experience, he or she will expand upon the best practices of that mentor, taking them, using them, and eventually putting a unique stamp on them. In the ideal world, this is a cycle as the new teacher slowly but surely becomes a veteran and, in turn, a mentor. It is a process that impacts children exponentially.

A+ Educators is about those who have been recognized on the state and national level over the past few years and includes profiles of sixty K–12 public schoolteachers. These are the trendsetters of the new century who are using innovation and technology, good old-fashioned common sense, and all available resources to deliver the best possible education to their students. And just as they mentor new teachers in their respective districts, these A+ educators will mentor the reader by virtue of sharing the tricks of their trade.

The profiles are diverse in that they cover teachers from all fifty states and from all grade levels, including teachers of the arts, special education teachers, and those who work with English-language learners and in vocational and technical education. Each profile is relatively similar in its construction, but variety comes in the kinds of units these teachers design, the way they use their experiences to help others, and their personal and professional backgrounds. Some of these A+ educators knew from childhood that they would teach, while many others had different careers before discovering their calling in education. On that note, several of these profiles reveal teachers who are as talented in their lives outside of school as they are in the classroom. There are plenty of authors, a couple of motivational speakers, and even some marathon runners and mountain climbers. There are people who once served in the Peace Corps and folks who have used summer vacations to travel the world. A common theme to all of these exploits is service to others, be it through fund-raising or international aid, and as one reads, it becomes obvious that the A+ educators are also A+ people.

Included here are several National Teachers of the Year (NTOY). This is an annual honor bestowed upon one state teacher of the year, and it culminates with a Rose Garden ceremony with the president. The Chief Council of State School Officers (CCSSO) oversees the selection process, and its National Selection Committee, composed of representatives from fourteen national education organizations, meets to choose four finalists and then, in February, selects the winner. The committee looks for teachers who inspire students of all backgrounds and abilities; who have the respect of students, parents, and colleagues; who are active in the community and within the school; who can withstand "a taxing schedule," as the CCSSO Web site states; and who are articulate enough to spend a year traveling the country talking to various groups about the state of education in the United States.

Prior to the national selection process, most states use a similar method to select their teacher of the year, although there are some subtle differences. In Alabama, for example, students, teachers, and administrators can submit nominations, and this seems to be the norm in most states. In Colorado, after nominations have been accepted, the candidate must submit a written application, an endorsement from the district, and letters of recommendation; open her or his classroom to committee visits; and give personal interviews. In Pennsylvania, a committee of former winners and finalists picks twelve semifinalists from a list of thirty nominees. Then the committee meets with personnel from the Pennsylvania Department of Education to choose a winner. Some states have multiple winners. For instance, in Arkansas, up to sixteen teachers may be recognized as regional teacher of the year. Those teachers receive various prizes, many of which are funded by the Walton Family Foundation. Another supporter of teacher of the year programs in several states is SMART Board, which makes whiteboards available to winners. Dell also gives away laptops, but the best prize seems to be a year's use of a convertible BMW for South Carolina's winner. That state's announcement is always exciting, as the entire process is anonymous. Louisiana's list of criteria is similar to most states in that it includes evidence of skills, certifications, detailed plans to continue in the profession, the ways in which respect for students, parents, and colleagues is demonstrated, leadership in the community, including community service, affiliation with professional educational organizations, knowledge of education policy, and the ability to inspire students of diverse backgrounds and abilities to learn. Some states are more influenced than others by the CCSSO criteria. Either way, in the end good teaching is good teaching!

Another matter that seems consistent from state to state is what concerns today's most talented educators. In the application process, the nominees are asked to name a critical issue and to offer a solution. As schools try to adjust to the new century, the two issues that trouble teachers more than any other are: (1) keeping kids in school, and (2) keeping new teachers in their schools. For reasons known and unknown, too many kids are dropping out of school. And for reasons known, but with no known solution, too many new teachers are leaving the profession. According to the National Commission on Teaching and America's Future, one third of all newly hired teachers leave during their first three years and almost half leave during the first five years. On the other side of the desk, statistics show that one student decides to leave high school every 29 seconds. One job of secondary schools is to prepare students for employment and self-sufficiency, and when that mission fails, a burden is placed on society. According to silentepidemic.org, the adult that has not graduated from high school will lose out on one million dollars in wages over the course of his or her lifetime. In turn, that means $9,000 less, annually, in tax revenue. When new teachers quit, it becomes nearly impossible for schools to develop and retain highly qualified A+ educators. This is especially true in districts with high rates of free and reduced-price lunch students. Just as the teacher-mentor cycle can make a positive impact on students, so too can the brain drain of disillusioned teachers have an exponentially negative effect. It's at this point that this problem becomes more than just an educational issue; it becomes a socioeconomic crisis.

In overwhelming numbers, the A+ educators presented in this book feel that good teaching is the great equalizer. Sure, more funding would help, but put a quality educator in front of a roomful of kids and good things are going to happen. Put a well-supported veteran in the classroom and watch good become great! The intention of *A+ Educators* is to entertain teachers and to maybe even inspire a few to reach for the highest of heights; it is to invite the general public into the classroom so that they can learn about some of the wonderful things that kids are doing under the care and guidance of their teachers; it is to let stories of the recent past help shape the future. These are times of great hope and *A+ Educators* is evidence that this hope is as substantial as a good grade and just as worthy of celebration. Let the learning continue.

Randy Howe
Madison, Connecticut
November 2008

You Are Entering the World of a Child:
Alabama's Betsy Rogers

Educational Philosophy

"Children, like rosebuds, bloom at different times. However, the last bloom is just as pretty as the first." Betsy learned this quote from her first-grade teacher, and she still abides by it today. Her dedication to each individual student stands as a shining example for teachers everywhere.

Dr. Helen Elizabeth "Betsy" Dawes Rogers is a woman who knows how to set the tone. The greeting "You are entering the world of a child . . ." is the first thing visitors see as they approach her classroom. This is the first line of a poem, and it speaks volumes about the regard Betsy has for her students.

"I believe the teacher must embrace the whole child in a caring and positive manner for learning to occur," she says. "The classroom environment should foster a climate that provides children with experiences that assist in developing the whole child. I also believe that the teacher must acknowledge the varying pace of each child's development." This holistic approach led to her recognition first on the state level and then on the national level when she was named the 2003 National Teacher of the Year. Betsy was even invited to meet President George W. Bush, and her TOY ceremony was held in the White House's Rose Garden.

Betsy has always taught in Alabama, beginning in 1974 at Hewitt Elementary School, and continuing to the time of her award at Leeds Elementary School. Learning about her craft included efforts in school as well as after school. She says that the work she did in her doctoral program "nurtured leadership skills I didn't know I had" and adds, "As a professional, I believe I should set an example of lifelong learning by continuing to seek improvement of my own teaching skills and by being knowledgeable about current research and trends in my field."

In 2000 she earned her certification from the National Board for Professional Teaching Standards. No doubt, this helped prepare her for the rigors of doctoral studies. Applying for board certification and writing a dissertation contributed to the quality of her teaching, and she unapologetically states that the key to improving our education system is training "master teachers with a heart for at-risk children who want to make a difference." This standard certainly applies to her.

Eleven years into her career, Betsy moved to Leeds Elementary, where she was overwhelmed by the problems many of the children faced, including abuse and neglect. Nevertheless, she was up for the challenge of breaking the cycle of poverty in that part of Alabama. Betsy explains, "I wanted to change the world for them. It took me several years to realize I could not change the world in which my students lived. But by understanding that school was the best place for some of my children, I became committed to making my classroom a place where students feel safe as well as creating an environment that provides joy to those with unfortunate lives."

In an age of high-stakes testing and work sheets, Betsy proved her educational mettle by designing a theme-based curriculum for her students. The kids could get comfortable knowing that for a week or maybe even a month, a good part of every day would be spent doing a related activity. One such theme was the Middle East, in which the class learned about animals that live in the desert and about the tents nomads use. The children displayed their artistic skills with a desert mural and "magic carpet art," and they revealed their theatrical talents when they dressed up in Middle Eastern costumes. There was a Middle Eastern feast and, as if that wasn't enough, Betsy encouraged the kids to write diary entries and create a personal passport as a means of teaching about the countries of the Middle East. Written expression, reading for comprehension, geography—it was all there. This was fun, but it wasn't just *for* fun.

Imagine the joy of these first-graders when Betsy told them she would be looping with them the following year to serve as their second grade teacher. It was an idea that required hours of thought, research, planning, and proposals from this amazing teacher. Long before looping became common, Betsy spent a year finding out about this new concept, gauging its repercussions while noting its benefits. At the end of that year, Betsy decided that looping was a worthwhile endeavor, so she submitted a proposal to her principal, and the board approved her request. This kind of innovative thinking earned Betsy the respect of her peers and the recognition of the president of the United States.

Dr. Bobby Neighbors, superintendent of Jefferson County schools, describes Betsy as "one of those extraordinary naturals for whom teaching is not only her vocation, it is her joy, her daily discovery, and her avocation. She can take the reluctant reader, the scared or shy student, and the sad, pitiful one from a dysfunctional home and, through her talents, find those subtle ways to build the confidence of the child as she helps him or her begin the journey of unlocking the potential within."

Only by entering the world of a child can one see all the potential within. For some children it is more difficult to find and unleash that potential. Sometimes the problem is a learning disability or a language barrier, and sometimes it is an accident of birth and economics. That's why Betsy is an advocate for equity in America's schools. She knows the value of research and cites indisputable data. "The federal government funds less than 7 percent of elementary and secondary education. Therefore, funding is left up to the individual state, and there is quite a large gap among the states concerning per-pupil spending." In checking the books of the General Accounting Office, Betsy learned that "more money was spent in wealthy districts than poor districts in thirty-seven states despite federal and state efforts to narrow funding gaps between poor and rich districts." In the same study, it was found that more often than not poorer districts try harder to raise money than wealthier districts. She explains, "Poor districts in thirty-five states made greater efforts to increase educational taxes than wealthy districts." When school budgets are passed, teachers can be hired and mentors can begin turning new teachers into master teachers. When state aid goes to needy districts, class sizes can be reduced and teachers are able to give students the individual attention they deserve. Throughout her career, Betsy has worked toward understanding her students and meeting them on their level, which is why she is an A+ educator.

—— Advice for Teachers New and Experienced ——

According to Betsy, every teacher should try to "find the best methods and materials for each child to master needed skills as well as aid in social and emotional development."

Down On the Farm:
Mississippi's Lee J. James

Educational Philosophy

I continually strive to develop teaching methods that will fit the needs of my students' learning styles while maintaining a level of teaching that does not bore more gifted students.

Legendary quarterback and future Hall of Famer Brett Favre made big news when he left the Green Bay Packers for the bright lights of New York City in 2008. He might be property of the Jets during the season, but the minute it ends, anyone who knows Favre knows that he catches the first flight south to his farm in Mississippi. Favre was raised in the town of Kiln, fondly referred to by its residents as "The Kill." There were no paved roads there when he was growing up; not one stoplight. This is bayou country. This is a land of fertile soil where John Deere could earn a vote or two if his name appeared on a ballot. This is where Lee J. James plies his trade.

Lee was the state's teacher of the year in 2007, and he did it as a teacher in a field that most Americans don't think of when discussing education and what classes their children are taking. Lee teaches agriculture power and machinery operations to sophomores, juniors, and seniors at the Choctaw County Career and Technology Center. Despite the requirements of No Child Left Behind, vocational education is still a vital part of many school districts, and Lee is an exemplary vo-ag teacher. His efforts are appreciated by local businesses, as vocational schools are often the feeder system for these businesses, and by kids who prefer hands-on learning. Pen-and-paper tasks aren't for everyone, and not all of today's students like to work on computers either.

The president of the National Association of Agricultural Educators, Lee has been involved in agricultural education for nineteen years. Thirty years before receiving his statewide award, he graduated from the Agricultural and Extension Education program at Mississippi State University. Fast forward to 2007, Favre's final year with the Packers, and Lee is still at it. In that year, he was named teacher of year, as well as winning the Mississippi Association for Career and Technical Education Outstanding Member Award. What Favre has been to the Packers, Lee has been to Choctaw Tech. Unlike Favre though, Lee is still there.

When asked about the biggest problem facing today's schools, and their students, he doesn't need to give his answer much thought. Lee actually articulates two problems that, hand-in-hand, are having a negative effect on America's schools. Lee says, "The most critical issues facing educators today are twofold, one being student apathy and the other being student dropout. Our students have become complacent about their studies and often drop out of school because of boredom or because they think things are better out in the world. . . . We, as educators, must encourage our students on a daily basis to develop their talents and commit themselves to getting the best education possible. Creative ways of teaching will help keep students interested and dedicated to learning."

Rather than fret over test scores and standardized tests, Lee gets down to the basics. "We must encourage students to stay in school," he says, "and get an education that will help make them productive citizens." He is certainly an educator who has his priorities in order. Lee understands accountability and knows better than to give all the credit to or place all the blame on the teacher. "Students have as much responsibility as the educators in their schools. . . . Students need to be prepared to enter each classroom with the attitude that they are going to learn something that day."

Still, the horse needs to be led to the water. And when working with kids more interested in puttering around under the hood than putting their thoughts into a five-paragraph essay, this can be a difficult task. Factor in that oftentimes special-needs learners are the ones attracted to this kind of alternative setting, places where talk is of agriculture and mechanics rather than reading, writing, and 'rithmetic, and one begins to see just how much work Lee had to do to produce such high-quality results.

Mississippi might be known for its bayou and its farmland, but with the likes of Lee and Favre, it should also be known for the quality of the professionals it produces. For bringing a sense of professionalism to his blue-collar branch of secondary education, Lee James is teaching's version of a Hall of Famer. He is an A+ educator.

Compliments to the Teacher

In 2003, Lee won one of the National Association of Agricultural Educators teacher mentor awards. Of Lee, the NAAE wrote, "Mentoring is something that Lee James does subconsciously. Lee has been an agriculture teacher for 25 years and has the experience to guide new teachers on their journey to becoming successful agricultural educators... When reviewing the curriculum, Lee provides his ideas and theories, but encourages his protégés to continually look for better ways to present the curriculum and to not settle with his ideas. Although Lee has taught for quite a while, he keeps an open mind, knowing that there may be something better along the way."

Learning from Elders and Northern Pike, Too:
Alaska's Ina B. Bouker

There's decoding and then there's reading for comprehension. And if Ina B. Bouker knows one thing, it's that reading for pleasure increases as comprehension increases; that to lay the foundation for a lifelong love of literacy, her first-graders need to know the basics. And then some.

Ina's motivation for teaching grew out of an early run-in with *Dick and Jane*. "Years back, when I was a young student, I would read over and over again the *Dick and Jane* stories. I was very good at reading the words, but if you had asked me what I was reading, I probably wouldn't answer the question. Why wouldn't I answer? Because even though I was reading fluently, I had no idea what a farm was, or even why the dog was living inside the house with the strange-looking yellow-haired people or what the cat was. No clue!"

Building vocabulary in students is important, especially if they come from homes that are not print-rich, where the TV is on more than books are opened, or where caregivers are so busy that the children aren't exposed to the kind of dialogue as their more advantaged peers. So for Ina it is important to build vocabulary and comprehension by explaining concepts the best she can. She wants struggling students to be able to relate, on some level, to what the class is reading. And the reading is not just in language arts; the attempt to build literacy is evident in all subjects.

So relate they do. In Alaska, Ina taps into Eskimo cultures to create lessons that the students can connect to. She even uses some of her own culture. "It is fun to creatively integrate curriculum with art, music, drama, languages, and cultures—especially my culture that I grew up with: the Eskimo Yup'ik culture."

No matter their backgrounds, most first-graders are intrigued, if not thrilled, by insects. And Ina uses bugs to describe one of her favorite accomplishments. A unit whose focus was originally insects ended up changing a little as Ina accommodated her kids' curiosity. Since Alaska's northern pike eat insects, she decided to teach some lessons on that local fish. When the class dissected one she had caught over the weekend, the children found other fish, a mouse, and even a small bird in its belly. The kids were hooked.

"I demonstrate, through this unit and others, that learning is fun, just as it should be!" Ina proudly proclaims.

With this new aquatic focus, Ina was able to teach the students (and keep in mind that these were first-graders) about the Alaskan water system. She taught them how to dissect and about the role of the stomach in the digestive system. They learned how to cut the pike, dry it, and add wild cranberries to make *akutaq,* a featured dish at Yup'ik celebrations. Ina could justify all these lesson plans because the students were learning so much, so she has repeated the unit with other classes. "I instruct as I use the Internet to share information on pike. We create an art project of a pike in its environment or habitat. We write about the pike . . . and display the project for the whole school to see." They read books on pike and she tells them a traditional story, hoping to teach them like the Yup'ik elders once taught their young with stories.

Just as Ina remembers the lesson of *Dick and Jane,* she uses what she learned from the elders to teach her students about social skills. "Frequently I tell my students of the elders who came into my school when I was in elementary school," she says. "They told us that we must be cautious *always* of how we want to be. . . . They would tell us how we should be careful of our decisions, because making decisions is a lifelong skill. I can still hear the elders saying to us that we must learn how to make decisions! They would repeat over and over, time and time again, that in order for us to do this, we must first learn to listen, follow directions, and learn to follow the rules."

In 2007 Ina was named the state teacher of the year for her work at Dillingham Elementary School, partly because she focuses not just on curriculum, but on life skills as well. She says, "Children are being raised without many of the social skills we would expect, because of changes in our families and society over the last few generations. Many of the children lack the ability to cooperate with their parents, teachers, and peers." For this reason she emphasizes social skills. Ina knows how important it is for kids to learn at a young age how to peacefully coexist with others. "One change is that many extended and immediate families do not live in close proximity to each other. Children are affected by divorce and living between two households, frequently thousands of miles apart. Many children are living in foster care or with relatives. Many parents lack the ability to teach positive social behaviors to their own children. They themselves did not learn the skills and therefore are not teaching the positive social skills. Our children are spending way too much time unaccompanied or in solitude. We want children to develop into productive members of our society. Children without positive social skills grow up with problems developing meaningful relationships, as well as behaviors that may lead to alcohol, drugs, violence, jail, and even death."

There is a way to teach these skills, however. "Children need creative play activity to learn how to set limits, negotiate, compromise, and learn each other's rights. Our children need guidance with interpersonal skills. Knowing empathy, sensitivity, and friendship skills helps students to communicate effectively. Our diverse students need advice or counseling in cultural competence. Cultural competence involves knowledge of and being comfortable with people of different cultural, racial, and ethnic backgrounds. Our students need training in resistance skills. Those include being able to defy negative peer pressure and dangerous community influences. Ultimately, we want our children to be raised with basic human values. We want children to celebrate each success as they accomplish goals and learn self-discipline to create an orderly way of life."

Noticeably absent from this description is punitive action. In Ina's classroom there is no corporal punishment, not one word about a time-out chair, nobody writing one hundred times "I will not do this" or "I will not do that" for homework. The difference is that Ina is proactive rather than reactive. She is a teacher rather than a disciplinarian.

"In general, I do not believe that I must control children, either by conditioning them with rewards and punishments or by meeting all of their 'needs.' I deal with discipline by asking questions in a quiet, courteous, respectful tone. If the student is willing to answer the questions, then the questions act as a teaching guide. He learns to think through the conflict with which he is dealing and tries to come up with ways to achieve his goals without violating the rights of others. In this way, a student also perceives me as noncritical and non-controlling. As my students consider the unintended consequences of their actions, they learn to make plans such that, whatever they decide to do, their actions carry with them the intent to respect the rights of others." They respect the rights of others, in no small part because their teacher respects their rights.

Ina is not old, but clearly she has the wisdom of an elder. And she receives the respect of an elder as well. That's why, when it comes to literacy skills and social skills, Ina can be counted among the A+ educators.

A Defining Moment

Ina remembers that when the elders would talk to her and her friends about their behavior, they would say, "No matter where we go, there will always be rules. There is no way out of rules but the wrong way."

Yo Quiero Triunfar *(I Want to Triumph)*: Arkansas's Justin Minkel

———— *In His Own Words* ————

¡Adelante, siempre adelante! ("Onward, ever onward!")

In 2007 Justin Minkel was named teacher of the year in Arkansas. Better yet, he was chosen by the Council of Chief State School Officers as one of four finalists for National Teacher of the Year. But believe it or not, this was not his most memorable moment as a teacher.

Justin says, "When I asked the seventh-graders to write about their goals for our summer program for at-risk English learners, I expected something along the lines of 'Get better at reading,' or 'Learn more math.' Marco, who arrived in Houston from Cuba one day before the program began, wrote one line: *Yo quiero triunfar en este país* ('I want to triumph in this country'). It struck me then that English learners' first experience of a foreign language and a foreign culture is deeply shaped by their first experience of school." Continuing to recall the more memorable moments of his professional career, Justin talks about his first year teaching second grade: "At the beginning of second grade in 2004, seventeen of my twenty-five students were below grade level in reading as measured by the Developmental Reading Assessment. By the end of my second year with these students, in May 2006, only three of the seventeen students were below grade-level; fourteen had reached or surpassed grade-level expectations in reading." Meeting the president of the United States on behalf of all the teachers in your state is nice, but according to Justin, it pales in comparison to teaching children how to read. Clearly he has his priorities in order!

For three of the four years that Justin was a student at Cornell University, he worked in a local elementary school. By the time he was a senior, Justin had rallied a group of thirty tutors to help out. After graduating, he signed on with Teach for America and was sent to a fourth-grade classroom in New York City. He stayed for two years before moving back home to Arkansas. Incredible success soon followed as he won the Milken Family Foundation National Educator Award in 2006. This came after being named a Flanders Fellow, in both 2003 and 2004, for his commitment to disadvantaged students. In 1998 he had won a fellowship with the America Reads Challenge Literacy Leadership program. Talk about success building upon success! Justin also received a Project Arts grant and co-researched a project that focused on student assessment in the area of fractions. He is truly a Renaissance man motivated to be the best teacher he can be.

Although reading, writing, and 'rithmetic are still in, Justin cites a few new Rs as guiding principles in his classroom. High standards and expectations translate to rigor, the first new R. The second is relevance, which allows the students to make a connection between their world and whatever concept they are studying. Finally—and this would seem to be an area of real strength for Justin—the third R stands for relationship. All teachers know the game is won or lost depending on the kind of relationship they cultivate with their students. Justin doesn't stop there, though. He has improved upon the three Rs with a fourth, about which he says, "My friends who teach art and music remind me to include richness—immersion in all the color and passion of literary and artistic works, some that reflect their culture and some that are as foreign to me as to them."

His classroom isn't all artwork and relation-building, though. In the age of No Child Left Behind, he supports the use of assessments to gauge student progress and to drive his instruction. However, the political side does concern Justin. "Accountability, based on quantitative data of student performance, is essential. Yet the tools for evaluation of student performance, the analysis of data, and the consequences of 'high-stakes' testing are often troubling, particularly when they are politically rather than educationally motivated." He continues, "I believe that it is my job as a teacher to enable students to both expand the range of options open to them and to choose among those options."

And what do the students have to say about all this? They bring it back to basics. "Mr. Minkel read us lots of great books and because of that, I love to read," exclaims Brian, a former student. "The best book that I remember was *The BFG* by Roald Dahl. After that, I started to read all of that author's books. Mr. Minkel read it like he was in the book with lots of expression. He even dressed up like the BFG! Mr. Minkel is the most amazing person I have known in my entire life. He is very smart, cool, lots of fun, and much, much more. He is my hero."

"His commitment to his students and the wider education community is, in one word, inspiring," says Arkansas Senator Mark Pryor. "As a result of high expectations and creative instruction, Minkel's students excel well beyond their grade level and are encouraged to exercise their knowledge. Justin has proven not only to be a great teacher, but also an outstanding citizen." As a citizen and teacher, Justin has a particular interest in those students who are English-language learners. He looks at them not with sympathy but with a methodical eye. He has worked hard to figure out how these students learn and what he can do to help them compensate. "We know that English learners, like most kids, tend to get more chances in school to be receptive than to be expressive. I make Writers' Workshop a central, daily event in my second-grade classroom, with a literary magazine we produce once a month. . . . If we're going to prepare our ELL students for twenty-first-century America, we need to link best practices for English-language learners with technology, and we need to use that technology in a way that addresses the full spectrum of twenty-first-century skills, including problem-solving, design skills, and higher order thinking." On the Internet, Justin has found a wonderful resource, one he likes so much that he even recommends it to the parents. "The best Web site I know of for families is *¡Colorín Colorado!* The site is bilingual," he explains, "so it helps to eliminate one of the two pieces of that double barrier that many Spanish-speaking families face: the language divide and the digital divide."

Dr. Jim Rollins, superintendent of the Springdale School District, has this to say about his award-winning teacher: "He has engendered the deep respect and affection of the students and their families, and the great rapport he has developed with them helps him to teach the children to high levels." The principal of Jones Elementary School, Debbie Flora, adds, "Mr. Minkel guides the students' learning by differentiating instruction so that truly 'no child is left behind.' He has established a classroom of learners that support each other."

When Justin was named Arkansas's teacher of the year, Governor Mike Huckabee commented, "Mr. Minkel has managed to take students who have shown difficulties in achievement and turned them into some of the state's most eager learners. His ability to inspire students who are lower income and for whom English is a second language is impressive and makes him very deserving of the Teacher of the Year Award."

Despite this kind of high-powered praise, Justin told the Associated Press, "Some people see teaching as a step in a career ladder and think if you're really good you'll definitely become a principal or a superintendent. I don't see it that way. I see teaching as a lifelong craft." Part of the reason for making it a long-term journey is to push oneself to greater and greater heights. This is an expectation that Justin also has of his students. "I expect a level of effort, critical thinking, and academic excellence from every child in my class that might seem more appropriate to a Gifted and Talented program or elite private school."

In Justin's private endeavors, the expectations are also high. So are the results. "As a drummer in a rock and blues band called Villa Incognito, I have raised money for New Orleans musicians left destitute by Hurricane Katrina as well as evacuees who chose to relocate to my town after the disaster. At a global level, I am involved in Oxfam, an organization to fight worldwide poverty in developing countries, and Res Publica, an organization to raise awareness of the current genocide in the Darfur region of the Sudan in East Africa." Justin also likes to write, including two unpublished novels and frequent letters to the editor, when the spirit moves him. Philanthropy is where he puts most of his time, though, volunteering for organizations like Project for Victims of Family Violence, a battered women's shelter.

With all the time he spends giving to others, one might wonder how much is left for his wife and daughter at home. Back in the Cornell days, a teacher taught him that he could have his cake and eat it, too. "I realized I wanted to become a teacher during my second year of college, when I worked in the classroom of an exemplary fourth-grade teacher. I felt the same respect for his knowledge and craft that I felt toward my college professors, and I saw in his example the kind of father, husband, and citizen I wanted to be. He had a balance in his life that I had not seen in other professionals as passionate and dedicated to their craft; he gave himself fully to his students, but he also made time for his son and daughter, and he balanced the intensity of the school years with summers spent on his farm in the country, harvesting garlic bulbs and taking walks with his children."

After winning teacher of the year, Justin was on sabbatical with the state Department of Education. For a year he worked with teachers across Arkansas, but once his leave came to an end, Justin was right back where everyone expected him to be: in the classroom. And with this kind of dedication, there can be no doubt that Justin Minkel is an A+ educator.

— Advice for Teachers New and Experienced —
My high school principal, John Delap, always said, "Think well and do good."

Mr. Accountability:
Georgia's Andy Baumgartner

────────── *Compliments to the Teacher* ──────────

"Andy's attention to his young students, his enthusiasm for their uniqueness and creativity, and his connection with their families merit his recognition as a national representative of teachers."

—Gordon Ambach, executive director of CCSSO

The Council of Chief State School Officers (CCSSO) is responsible for naming the National Teacher of the Year. Its members seek the best of the best while also trying to find teachers from all different disciplines and grade levels. In 1999 the CCSSO recognized Andy Baumgartner and in doing so, achieved its goal of diversity. Andy is a rare breed, after all—a man who teaches kindergarten.

But make no mistake. Andy was not chosen simply because his position is uncommon. He deserves all the accolades. The first winner from Georgia, and only the second kindergarten teacher to win the award, Andy teaches at A. Brian Merry Elementary School. In 1999, not only was he honored by President Bill Clinton, but he also won a Milken Award. At the time of these national awards, Andy had been teaching for twenty-three years.

Over the years he has developed an agreeable notion of what a classroom ought to look like. He says it "should be a place where each child's needs for understanding and attention are understood and met, where they feel loved and treasured, and where there is a definite set of boundaries that are clearly stated and consistently enforced." He adds, "I must make every effort to challenge the stronger students to strive toward further progress and to patiently love the struggling students into persevering. Through the use of encouragement, praise, and the spotlighting of individual successes, I can promote self-confidence and self-worth, and a feeling of accomplishment at each level of instruction for each student."

When asked what the biggest challenges facing America's schools are, he listed one within the classroom and one outside it. In his opinion, the two greatest challenges are "successfully meeting the needs of each student and upgrading the public's perception of our integrity as a profession." The way to meet both of these challenges is with accountability. Andy embraces that notion, starting with his own personal responsibilities. "I must be held accountable for making certain that the children in my classroom experience every opportunity to learn to trust educators and to develop a joy of learning! I must also be held accountable for instilling in them the proper conduct and citizenship skills that will enable them to positively contribute to the creation and continuation of a classroom environment that promotes individual student achievement and the productivity of a school. . . . I must consciously strengthen my emotional and mental health, avoid prejudice and stereotyping, and maintain a high level of energy to possess the stamina needed to meet the challenges of students and career."

Filling out report cards or receiving test scores from the state can be important moments for teachers to reflect on their own accountability. They certainly are for Andy. Analyzing the data, he looks at what he did with a particular group of students and then he looks forward. "Because I am always aware of my competence as an educator," he says, "I am intent on tracking the progress of my students as they leave me so that I might change and upgrade my approach and enhance my effectiveness." Communicating with other teachers is a key to success as well. "No one sets higher standards for students or higher accountability for teachers than effective teachers do—for it is teachers who suffer the most from a lack of accountability. An ineffective teacher on the grade level below is a poor base on which to build. An ineffective teacher on the grade level above is work and time gone to waste." When teachers work as a team, accountability can be a friend and not a foe.

"The biggest kick in teaching," Andy says, "comes when I look into the face of a young child and watch confusion turn to concentration, concentration to surprise, and finally surprise into the pride of accomplishment." This is what Andy calls his finest moment as a teacher. "Every student has a right to find some element of success in his or her school career, since this is most often the major prerequisite to finding success in life."

For Andy, finding success has everything to do with finding a way to help others. His father was a minister who taught Andy and his five siblings that helping others "was one way of paying back all of the blessings that were placed in our lives." And it was his mother who taught them all "how to be nurturers. She encouraged me to be true to myself and that gentleness and consideration of others can be masculine as well as feminine traits." What parent wouldn't want to hear that from their child's teacher?

Teaching is personal for Andy, and the idea of service is still a part of his home life today. His wife is a principal, and he has two children who are exceptional learners. "Having a son with a learning disability and an attention deficit allows me to see my profession from an additional perspective. I understand the feelings of frustration, heartache, and even anger that many parents suffer when they feel that the system is too large or too uncaring or just not capable of helping their children with educational success." There are other issues in schools he would like to see addressed. "As the father of an above-average son of sixteen, I have been made aware of the importance that extracurricular activities such as drama, band, and chorus can make in developing positive attitudes about school and how well they lend themselves to building skills and characteristics important to scholarship. I have also been exposed to the unfortunate way in which those programs are forced to take a backseat to athletics and are rarely funded or supported equally by our schools and communities."

Andy also recognizes how hard his fellow teachers are working. "I am in the remarkable position of having observed firsthand that our profession is filled with intelligent, talented, energetic, creative, and nurturing individuals who believe in themselves and in the children they teach and are enthusiastically optimistic about the possibilities for the future."

In addressing the stamina needed to make it through a school year, he advises, "I would remind teachers of how important it is to have a life outside of teaching. It is imperative to establish relationships with family and friends that can offer strength and support; it is important also to spend ample time enjoying leisure activities. Our students deserve happy, well-rounded, rested, and exuberant adults to teach and care for them!" That advice applies to all teachers. For the newbies, in particular, he says, "The effective teacher always considers the needs of his or her students first! The truly successful teacher knows and cares about students as individuals and worthy members of a school community. The well-balanced teacher is equally adept at planning, instructing, evaluating, remediating, and enriching. The motivating teacher makes learning relevant, exciting, and fun. The beloved and remembered teacher instills in students an unquenchable thirst for learning and a resilient desire for success. The happy, healthy teacher finds joy in the work and in family, hobbies, and other pursuits outside of teaching." To achieve all of these is a daunting task for new teachers, but worth pursuing nonetheless.

One of Andy's favorite quotes comes from Albert Einstein who said, "Creativity is more important than intellect." For combining the creative with the intellectual, for his tireless pursuit of accountability, and for teaching kindergarten when most men would run in the other direction at the sight of a room full of five-year olds, Andy gets an A+!

— *Advice for Teachers New and Experienced* —

I would encourage teachers to take an active part in the political processes that govern our schools and to resist the temptation to confine themselves to the four walls of their classrooms. There has never been a time when teacher voice and teacher activism were more needed or more important than they are right now.

Creating a Professional Learning Community for Parents and Colleagues: Maryland's Kimberly Oliver

To hear the name Broad Acres Elementary School is to picture a pastoral scene of education where all is calm and all is well. That vision is far more accurate today than in the past because Broad Acres, in Silver Spring, Maryland, is where Kimberly Oliver teaches kindergarten. She welcomes so many of the town's children to their first school experience. Those lucky enough to be in her class don't even know what it means to be the National Teacher of the Year, but this is exactly what Kim is, having been recognized with the honor in 2006.

Kim was the fifty-sixth National Teacher of the Year and the first from Maryland. She credits a daycare teacher she had as a child, as well as summers spent working at a camp, with paving her way to the classroom. "I realized that I adore working with children. This experience helped to shape many of my beliefs about what children can do if someone believes in them. I knew then that I wanted to motivate and inspire the neediest students whom many have written off just because of the circumstances they were born into."

Just six years before the president came knocking at Broad Acres' door, the school was close to being written off by the state. Due to declining academic performance, the threat of restructuring was very real. The teachers, including Kim, understood what they were up against, given that 90 percent of their students live in poverty and 75 percent speak a foreign language at home. The turnaround, though, came quickly. Within one year, Broad Acres was the number-one school in the district in terms of percentage increases on test scores. In 2003, 2004, and 2005 the team at Broad Acres met or exceeded all requirements of No Child Left Behind. How did they do it?

"By building a professional learning community and emphasizing collaboration, I have impacted the learning of more than five hundred students," Kim says of her role at Broad Acres. "Through collaborating with others, I helped turn around an underperforming school despite the obstacles of poverty, race, language, and mobility. . . . I am proud to be a teacher, and I work to strengthen and improve the teaching profession by training other educators. I do this because I believe that the quality of a child's teacher can be the most important factor in determining his or her success."

Ernie M. Cadet, the parent of two former students and a classroom volunteer, adds, "I saw for myself how much the students learned from Ms. Oliver, but I learned very much from Ms. Oliver also. I learned how I could help my own children at home; I learned that every parent, regardless of where they come from, what language they speak, or how much education they have themselves, can help their child and their school. It takes a special kind of teacher to draw that out of parents—a teacher like Ms. Oliver." Like his children, Ernie is an English-language learner, and they all have been learning together.

"She is interested in all of my family," Ernie says in praise. "She has helped us all in some way."

Diane Hoffman, the in-district trainer for the Montgomery County Public Schools, has witnessed firsthand the power of collaboration in Kim's classroom. "There is not one wasted minute of instructional time during any day. Together they create quite a symphony of learning." On top of that, says Dr. Jerry D. Weast, superintendent of schools, "she works with students in a way that allows them to flourish in an environment where their various cultures, languages, and experiences are respected."

All of this flourish and symphonic learning is a result of how hard Kim works to promote literacy in the community. She says, "I remember feeling empowered and independent when I became a reader." One effort she makes is to sponsor a Books and Supper Night four times a year. Families visit the school and check out books from its library. They read together, receive free books, and enjoy a dinner—all together.

Kim lets the ideas of togetherness, teamwork, and community guide much of what she does. She teaches the smallest students in the school, but they are all future citizens in her eyes. "As a teacher, I believe it is my duty to teach my students, the youngest community members, their civic role. I accomplish this through a thematic unit on communities and mini-lessons on various topics such as littering, gardening, and recycling."

Still, Kim understands how much more could be accomplished at Broad Acres with a more comprehensive program of school readiness; something like universal preschool or Head Start. When asked what the most important issue facing America's schools is, she replies, "Currently, parents pay the bulk of the expenses for preschool education. The quality of preschool programs varies depending on cost. Consequently, many of our neediest students are denied access to a quality early childhood education." But she is quick to add her definition. "Equity to me does not mean that each student receives the same instruction and completes the same task. Rather, I believe equity in a classroom means that each child receives exactly what he or she needs to move forward."

Kim is an experienced teacher with the kind of résumé to make a principal shake his or her head in wonder. Having graduated college just two years before arriving at Broad Acres, Kim now has a master's degree in elementary education. She is a National Board Certified Teacher and has mentored eleven colleagues while they too worked to become nationally certified. She is also a mentor at home, having decided to be the guardian to a teenage cousin whose father passed away. Does anyone doubt her cousin is in good hands? It would seem that Kim Oliver is an A+ cousin, just as she is an A+ educator.

Educational Philosophy

I want to motivate and inspire the neediest students, whom many have written off, and let them know that they can achieve and succeed in life regardless of what the statistics may show.

From Troop to Teacher:
Ohio's Eric A. Combs

——————— *Educational Philosophy* ———————

Eric knows that what his students ultimately get out of their education will be in proportion to what they put into it. He uses Shakespeare to explain. "'Every subject's duty is to the King, but every subject's soul is his own' from *Henry V*, William Shakespeare. In the modern vernacular, we all have duty in this world of education, but the student alone must shoulder their own education to whatever end they take it."

Once upon a time, Eric Combs taught students in fatigues. He was an instructor for the Air Force Junior Reserve Officers' Training Corps and delivered curricula on American history, military history, customs and courtesies, outdoor education, and orienteering/land navigation. On a more serious note, for twenty years he served in the U.S. Air Force Security Forces, often as a trainer.

Eric is a graduate of the U.S. Army Air Assault School and has made nineteen jumps, all from helicopters. He was stationed in South Korea, Kuwait, Saudi Arabia, Germany, Wyoming, and England, and deployed in the Middle East, North Africa, and Europe. And now he can tell the students at Fairborn High School in Fairborn, Ohio, all about it because Eric has made the leap from the Air Force to the classroom via a special program aimed at putting qualified teachers into Ohio's schools. Eric got his opportunity through Troops to Teachers, which is funded in part by an Expanding the Pool of Qualified Teachers grant. He now teaches social studies—and teaches it well.

In 2005 Eric earned his master's degree and in 2006, just as he was beginning an educational leadership program at Antioch University, he was named the Ohio Teacher of the Year. After three years as a civilian serving at Fairborn High, Eric had clearly bought into his newest mission. Still, he appreciates what the Air Force did for him, showing him the possibilities for a second career. He credits pure serendipity. "I believe it was passion and a bit of luck. . . . I once got a taste of teaching kids when I did a tactical demonstration for a bunch of high school students. I had a passion for what I did in the Air Force and now it seems I've enlivened that again in teaching."

Sticking with the military theme, Eric began a "school within a school" program at Fairborn called the Delta Team. The focus of the Delta Team is the school's most at-risk students, and the program has been deemed a success. "When a student knows that you set high standards, and when they know you care about them, I have found them to be magnificent achievers. . . . My philosophy is to bring students to that place of opportunity to learn, that spot in history or geography where they can feel free to ask 'why.' I challenge them to limit excuses and not allow the paltry habits of today to invoke the disease of apathy."

Although it is important to get kids excited about learning and invested in the idea of personal accountability, Eric also knows that when working with at-risk students, it is often prudent for the teacher to put his or her syllabus away until the student is ready. He says, "In order for me to be successful in the classroom, I must know my students and be willing to meet them where they are."

"Eric's passion for the classroom and devotion to his students is setting the standard for teaching at Fairborn High School and throughout the state," says Susan Tave Zelman, superintendent of public instruction in Ohio.

Eric's passion extends from his students to his colleagues. After all, his first career was built around teamwork, so sharing advice comes easily for him. "Be a role model for students, staff, and parents," he states. "Lead by example and try to make each day the best possible for your students. If something offends, don't join others in complaining, put your brain and muscles to work in fixing the issue and addressing how it affects the educational environment." What is the purpose, after all, of teamwork if not to solve problems? Sometimes when the problem takes place within the four walls of the classroom, the teacher, already feeling isolated, decides he or she must solve it within those four walls. Not true, Eric says. "Knock on the door of the teachers around you. Don't be a hermit and don't take it all on yourself. Find a mentor and master teacher to learn from and never be afraid to go back and try a lesson again. Finally, don't take it personal."

The other thing Eric hopes his colleagues will understand is that their problems aren't necessarily the same as those of their students. It's the old "walk a mile" allegory, and he knows it's possible for teachers to be demanding as well as understanding. "I believe adapting to our ever-changing social and political environment is a huge challenge to all educators. Knowing that our issues of the past may not be those of our students is a key element of understanding who we are as educators and who our students are as individuals, coming to us for help."

Passion like this is possible only when there is a heightened sense of appreciation. For Eric, that appreciation comes in part from a short stint he spent working as a factory manager in between arriving at Fairborn and his final days with the Air Force. His boss at the factory told him he had to fire a woman who was raising her granddaughter while her daughter was in prison. "I don't think I'll ever forgive myself for that," Eric says. "After I fired her, my boss put me in for a raise for doing it. I knew then that I was in the wrong spot." There are hundreds, if not thousands, of people in Fairborn, Ohio, who are happy Eric found the right spot.

One of Eric's skills is that he is a people person. He served with men and women from a wide variety of backgrounds, and that experience clearly has had an impact on his educational philosophy. For the life he has led and the decisions he has made, for the example he sets for his students, and for the help he gives his colleagues, Eric is a true A+ educator.

A student told Eric her brother was home from Iraq but couldn't answer his question as to what branch of the service he was in. "I don't know, he got some purple medal, though." He asked her to bring in the medal, and after presenting the Purple Heart Citation to the class, she broke down in tears and said, "My brother is a hero." Eric felt like everyone had learned something as a result of that teachable moment.

"This Place Looks Like Red Lobster": South Carolina's Jason Scott Fulmer

Compliments to the Teacher

"I believe the reasons Jason is such an outstanding young man can be summed up in three words: character, commitment, and compassion."

—Diedre M. Martin, assistant chancellor for external affairs at the University of South Carolina, Aiken

"There are an estimated thirty-seven thousand ways to make a living in the United States," says Jason Fulmer. "Whatever our chosen career, it is imperative that we stop looking at work as simply a means of making a living and realize it is an essential ingredient in making a quality life. Teaching is the essential profession, the one that makes all other professions possible." Three cheers to that!

"As a male elementary education major, I was a minority. Some people could not understand why I would want to choose education as a career path. They cautioned against my choice to become an educator," Jason recalls, not necessarily with fondness. "'It will be hard to support a family,' many advised. 'There are not many men in elementary schools; you can make more money with another career and just volunteer.' I wondered how many other men before me heard these types of statements and decided to pursue other avenues. Determined, I continued to pursue my calling and mission in life." That calling is to teach third grade at Redcliffe Elementary School in Aiken, South Carolina. Those third-graders should be happy Jason didn't listen to all the naysayers.

"Often I am the first male teacher that my students encounter. To analyze what they are anticipating, I have my kids write about what they expect from a male teacher. I ask them to write this at the beginning and at the end of the school year to see if their anticipations are accurate." According to research conducted by the National Education Association, only 9 percent of America's elementary school teachers are men. Jason's earliest urges, though, were not spurred on by politics or by turning conventional wisdom on its ear. No, Jason began teaching long before he could even read a newspaper or textbook. "My first students were Mickey and Snoopy. I taught them the alphabet with my child-sized chalkboard. Eventually my sister and the neighborhood kids chose me to be the teacher of the imaginary school in our living room. The teacher was my dream role to play and one I played often."

What his sister didn't realize was that her brother would go on to be the 2004 South Carolina Teacher of the Year. And those neighbors didn't realize they were being taught by a guy who would be a finalist for National Teacher of the Year.

Incredibly, Jason was recognized by the CCSSO after just four years in the classroom. Even more incredible is the résumé he has compiled in such a short time. For example, he is on the board of the South Carolina Association of Supervision and Curriculum Development and is a frequent presenter in the areas of teacher recruitment and mentoring. Even more impressive, Jason is pursuing national board certification. He's involved with his church's youth group and sings in the classroom, too. When students are struggling with rounding numbers, he busts out a modified version of the theme song "Moving on Up" from *The Jeffersons*: "Well, we're moving on up, up the number line. If it's five or higher we move on up the line."

On that note, Jason adds, "Creative lessons and strategies help students increase their mastery of skills, and if it means taking a commercial jingle that students hear daily and rewriting it to teach a math concept, I try it. Tossing a beach ball with literature questions printed on it engages my students to participate in the discussion of a story we are studying. History comes to life when I teach my students about the rich culture of South Carolina and teach them to shag, the state dance."

A love of the arts is often driven by dreams and of dreams, Jason says. "Our dreams act as compasses, illuminating the direction we should travel as we set a course of action for our lives. A dream gives us hope for the future and a vision for the present."

If you're envisioning a room full of dreamy quotes and cheesy songs, it's important to know that a sense of humor is at work here, as well. "This place looks like Red Lobster; I am going to love it," said a new student the first time he saw Jason's classroom beach theme. "You are the best teacher in the world," says a former student named Kychaun, "because you do fun activities that help us learn. When I grow up and become a teacher, I will do fun activities with my students."

Jason thinks it's important for his students to know his personality and that he cares about them. They'll all be working together for ten months, after all. "Schools should prepare students for life situations beyond the textbook and help them connect concepts with real-life experiences. The old saying 'Put your students in rows and do not smile until December' is indeed out of date when we must seek to build community and foster collaboration among our young people." Besides, it's hard to be inspirational if you frown all the time. A parent, Amy B. Poston, shares that "Mr. Fulmer's primary focus is clearly to inspire his students to be their best."

Jason's boss sees it that way, too. Dr. Teresa L. Pope, principal of Redcliffe Elementary School, says, "It has been my good fortune to work with Jason as his principal, to have my daughter in his classroom, and to have my son, who is an education major, observe and learn from him. Jason has proven himself as an outstanding educator through his dedication, knowledge, enthusiasm, compassion, and his ability to reach all children. His love for teaching and learning is contagious and he inspires not only his students but their parents, aspiring educators, and his colleagues as well."

When asked to comment on a critical issue in schools today, Jason says, "We must build continuity and stability in the lives of students by reducing the teacher turnover rate. Working conditions are the number-one reason teachers leave, according to the National Commission on Teaching. Schools must become learning communities that prosper in a spirit of collaboration. Maintaining a community of learners is paramount to the success of effective schools. Far too often, teachers are discouraged, fatigued, in danger of severe burnout, and leave the profession partly due to isolation. We all need renewal, but we have to keep that spark burning, be innovative, and willing to adapt with change. According to Marilyn Katzenmyer [University of South Florida, College of Education professor], 'Within every school there is a sleeping giant of teacher leadership, which can be a strong catalyst for making change.' By using the energy of teacher leaders as agents of social change, the reform of public education will stand a better chance of building momentum." In the past, Jason would have been that sleeping giant, but leadership in his building and district recognized that even though he is a relatively new teacher, he is a leader among his peers. Acting upon his concern, Jason is involved with the South Carolina Teacher Cadet program, which recruits high school seniors for teaching. He is also involved with the Center for Educator Recruitment, Retention, and Advancement.

Jason has become an A+ educator in less than five years' time. Who knows what he'll have achieved by his tenth year of teaching?

Educational Philosophy

One of my favorite stories as a young boy was *The Little Engine That Could*. My mom read the book to me often and encouraged me to always do my best. "I think I can" became a part of my daily vocabulary, fueling my desire and commitment to reach for my dreams.

A Highly Qualified Teacher:
Tennessee's Susanne H. Frensley

—— *Advice for Teachers New and Experienced* ——

Susanne's advice to new teachers is to remember that, "We are working with human beings, and things rarely go exactly as planned."

All of the A+ educators have incredible résumés, and some have had experiences that create a sense of envy and awe when one reads about them. Susanne Frensley, with her accomplishments and her experiences, is one such awe-inspiring educator.

In 2007 Susanne earned the teacher of the year award for Tennessee. She teaches history and art history at Hillsboro Comprehensive High School in Nashville, and her students have certainly benefited from their teacher's travels. After all, Susanne has taught art history in eight countries. At the time of her award, she had been teaching for thirteen years and 95 percent of her students had passed the Advanced Placement art history exam over the past nine years. Obviously, Susanne didn't just bring great stories home from abroad.

It is obvious how much Susanne's students love her class. They were the ones, after all, who initiated the teacher of the year process for her. After nomination, Susanne had the thrill of a lifetime when she was chosen to carry the Olympic torch on part of its journey through Tennessee.

Lana Seivers, the state's education commissioner, says, "Students respond when teachers show enthusiasm for their subject and genuine interest in the lives and success of their students. I congratulate Ms. Frensley on earning the esteem of her colleagues by demonstrating these qualities."

"It is important that each and every student feel honored in my classroom," Susanne believes. "I create a place where students can think freely and be themselves. Above all, I hope to support their intellectual curiosity and foster a love of the visual arts." She adds, "Teaching adolescents is an incredible opportunity to connect with children who are experiencing an inordinate number of physical, emotional, and social changes."

Recently, though, that opportunity was taken from Susanne for a time. Despite all the years of experience and that great pass rate on the AP exam, the stipulations of No Child Left Behind (NCLB) left her with no job. Specifically, it was the legislation requiring highly qualified teachers in every classroom that left Susanne without teaching certification. "This law has done some great things," she says. "But it is imperative that they team with teachers. Teachers need to be at the table." Susanne's story is just one example why greater teacher involvement in the creation of the legislation would be beneficial to everyone involved. Susanne can still teach, but under the new laws she is no longer considered highly qualified. Teachers from forty-one states have submitted a list of ten recommendations for improving NCLB. In regards to the "highly qualified" issue, their document reads, "We have to go beyond content knowledge to a teacher's proven effectiveness in raising student achievement."

In regards to those veteran teachers who serve as models to the kids as well as their fellow teachers, Susanne knows exactly what they do. She says they "respect and honor students, connect with the age group they are teaching, love the subject they teach, possess a sense of humor and the ability to laugh at oneself, have a high energy level, and make a commitment to students, regardless of who they are or where they are from." Sounds a lot like Susanne and her teaching style.

Out of commitment comes community, and in a properly constructed, effectively nurturing community, much can be achieved. "Learning time is precious," Susanne says, "and the deepest, most meaningful learning occurs when students have the opportunity to be creative with the concepts or material. When students feel safe to be creative in this nurturing, flexible environment, students go deep with creativity, and throughout the year their creativity blossoms."

One thing about teaching in a public school that Susanne enjoys is a diverse student body that must remind her of the world she once traveled. In any creative field, this is the life blood: different people contributing different ideas and perspectives. Hillsboro provides the diversity, and Susanne has figured out how to work with all those different learning types.

She says, "Diversity is paramount because every student brings something important to each class. Regardless of a student's skill or academic level, students are able to thrive in my classroom. Students who otherwise are considered behavior problems flourish because each of their creative talents are identified, celebrated, and harvested; their voices, thoughts, and opinions are indispensable to the success of the whole class. As a result, I have an inordinate number of 504, MIP Fragile and Behavior, Special Education, and Advanced Placement students together in the same classes."

Getting them into her class is one thing. Keeping them in school is another. "A critical issue facing educators today is the low percentage of public school students who graduate from high school," Susanne laments. "Currently only 60 percent of Metro Nashville Public School students graduate." The reasons for this are clear, at least in Susanne's mind. "A decrease in funding for guidance counselors remains a significant impediment to lowering the dropout rate. Systems must find ways to pair adults with at-risk students, whether through teacher advisory enterprises, mentoring programs, or volunteers from the community because research indicates that an invested adult/adolescent relationship is most likely to avert the decision to drop out. Failure to address low graduation rates compromises our national security as much as it impedes the ability of our children to both contribute to and share in national prosperity."

Susanne freely admits that she reaches out to all different kinds of kids when discussing the following year's Advanced Placement classes. She is the type of teacher who helps kids feel valued and welcome. She is the type of teacher who fights the dropout rate one student at a time. Her weapons are paintbrushes and pencils, compassion and good old-fashioned storytelling. For bringing the world into her classroom and for welcoming Nashville's children into that wider world for a little while each day, Susanne is an A+ educator—a highly qualified A+ educator.

Educational Philosophy

Susanne's biography, on the Tennessee education Web site, states that her art history "philosophy draws upon existing knowledge from a wide range of disciplines and merges current trends in art education, including Multiculturalism, Postmodernism, Visual Culture, and Post-Structuralism. The curriculum challenges students on a variety of levels simultaneously and effectively cultivates cognitive processing skills required to succeed in all areas of secondary education. Furthermore, students gain the knowledge and skills to recognize and confront the realities of their own cultures, while responding to issues of race, ethnicity, gender, sexuality, and socio-economic status."

A One-Man Carnival:
Massachusetts's Michael Flynn

Authentic learning relates to the real world, and when it comes to getting students excited about learning, Michael Flynn is the real deal.

Michael, a second-grade teacher in Southampton, Massachusetts, is known for creating authentic learning experiences for his students. When it was time to teach them about fish, he didn't make copies of a work sheet or ask students to open a textbook. Instead, he gave his class the opportunity to raise salmon, and the unit culminated with their releasing their fish into a local river. When Michael wanted to teach his students about air pressure, he had them design rockets. As you could probably guess, the final lesson involved launching those rockets. And when Michael wanted to teach his class about the media, his greatest idea yet came to fruition.

Michael was named the 2008 Massachusetts Teacher of the Year, partly because of the TV show he produces with his students throughout the school year. Once a unit of study is complete, the students work in small groups to develop skits, news reports, interviews, experiments, or whatever works best to highlight what they've learned. The show is then played throughout the school and shared with families. One such show, for example, was about Antarctica.

"When you walk into his class," Collins says with pride, "you see the children who are engaged. They are wrapped around his every word. Their parents say they all talk around the dinner table about what Mr. Flynn is doing."

Everybody remembers their best teachers, and it is clear that Michael earns that place in the world of each and every student. "If I can do it in a way that will create those lasting memories, that's how I do it," explains Michael.

The other teachers at Norris appreciate his efforts, as well. "Mike approaches teaching with a level of intellectual curiosity and commitment to the field of education that should be the standard for our profession," says Anne O'Reilly. "His infectious enthusiasm for teaching and natural leadership qualities, combined with his professional knowledge and skill make him a clear choice for Massachusetts Teacher of the Year."

Michael's enthusiasm is contagious and he is able to maintain it, even during potential disciplinary actions. A former student named David explains how his teacher runs his class: students have three chances otherwise, "you have to sit down and just watch, but you can still learn." Three strikes and you're out—kind of. David recalls another aspect of life in Michael's classroom. "If everyone works their hardest, we get a brain break," he says, smiling.

Michael knows that everybody needs a little rest every now and again, so he provides those "brain breaks." For example, he might do a magic trick for the kids, like the time he made a tissue disappear, then reappear. Everybody gets a break, except Michael!

"The nature of this job is to focus on the kids," he says. "We [teachers] are not looking for any kind of attention." On June 22, 2007, the day after Michael won his teacher of the year award, Javier C. Hernandez wrote in the *Boston Globe*, "To his students, Michael B. Flynn is a one-man carnival who uses funny voices and camcorders to bring life to spelling and subtraction. To his peers, he is a blazing young teacher with a zeal for reforming the way educators teach math."

"He's really nice, and we feel like we have a lucky teacher," says Jacqueline, a former student. "We wish he was a third-grade teacher so we could have him for another year."

The only kids who get to loop with Michael year after year are his four children. When not spending time with them, he contributes to DVDs and books on mathematics instruction and travels around the country running professional development sessions on the Investigations in Number, Data, and Space curriculum. When he isn't doing that work, he serves as a recreation commissioner for the City of Northampton and as a board member for the Northampton Education Foundation, which grants money to teachers.

It would seem that Michael has managed to create a thirty-hour day and an eight-day week. For figuring out how to squeeze so much in, and for using that time to better the lives of those around him, he is an A+ educator.

Compliments to the Teacher

At the ceremony to announce this honor, Education Commissioner David Driscoll said, "A good teacher can help students learn, but a great one can instill enthusiasm in every student."

Lattice Work:
Michigan's Margaret Holtschlag

In Her Own Words

Technology is simply a tool that we use when we learn, and my students are finding that it's a tool that they reach for more and more frequently, and with growing ease.

Over the years Margaret Holtschlag has called places all around the world "home." That's because in some ways the world is the greatest resource her classroom has, and she can tap into it through a variety of lessons, units, and adventures.

In 1999 Margaret spent the summer in South Africa, studying that country's culture and educational system. In addition, she established the first network of e-mail correspondence between students from the United States and rural Korea and then took twenty-three kids and parents to Korea. Margaret is a founding member of LATTICE (Linking All Types of Teachers to International Cross-cultural Education), which brings local educators, international students, and Michigan State University faculty together once a month to discuss education and diversity. Murphy Elementary School in Haslett, Michigan, might be home, but Margaret recognizes that she is a citizen of the world. So much of what she teaches helps her students realize the same about themselves.

An unfortunate opportunity to build empathy in people is through tragedy. When a natural disaster strikes another part of the world, it provides a chance to expose kids to circumstances they might not think about otherwise. Margaret believes that human beings are, in essence, good, so when, for example, there was an earthquake in Kobe, Japan, she was ready to have her students do what they could to help. They immediately launched a fund-raiser, making stickers featuring the friendship ideogram, which they learned about from a retired teacher who maintained a correspondence with friends in Japan. In three weeks' time, the students earned approximately $1,200—from stickers! They donated the money to the Red Cross's earthquake relief fund. Some time later, a Japanese professor who had heard of the class's efforts came to see the kids while visiting East Lansing. He came to say thank you and ended up sharing insight into his culture. Margaret was proud to see her idea come to fruition: helping others while using technology to provide a spontaneous learning environment for kids. Not to be lost in all this is the increasing presence of technology in schools and in the world in general, and the way Margaret tries to show the kids the benefits of this technology.

"Each experience that I plan for my students should have three key elements," she says, listing "significance, joy, and celebration. I know I can't achieve these elements in every lesson, but it is my driving goal."

To be an elementary school teacher is to be a generalist. One must possess a working knowledge of all subjects. That said, Margaret clearly likes topics related to social studies. In particular, she has a passion for museums, and much like her international interests, she has been able to turn this passion into an effective teaching tool. Margaret, who has taught all primary grades except kindergarten and third grade, is the teacher in residence at the Michigan Historical Museum. This is just one of the cherries on top of a teaching career that has spanned more than twenty years. She is pleased to still be in the classroom, as well as having the opportunity to deliver her museum curriculum, "One Big History Lesson," to a wider audience. Students come to the museum for five days and take part in creative lesson plans that combine artifacts, guest speakers, teachers, and hands-on learning.

In addition to her work with the museum, Margaret and her husband, a U.S. Geological Survey hydrologist, received an Excellence in Education grant from the U.S. Department of the Interior so they could do a multimedia project on wetlands. Margaret has cowritten nine editions of the *Random House Calendar for Kids,* as well as two children's books. She also has written a number of teachers' guides and articles about reading and science.

Writing is a passion, just like international studies, philanthropy, museums, and the environment, but Margaret admits that teaching is her lifelong passion. "I think I had always wanted to be a teacher," she recalls, "which started with doing stuff with my younger brothers and sisters." As one of twelve children, Margaret had plenty of "pupils."

Despite more than two decades in the classroom, Margaret still brings an immense sense of joy to her teaching. Over and over again, this has proven to be a contagious sentiment, mostly because Margaret constructs it that way. "When a student pursues learning just for the sake of learning, the joy is there. And that's a lifelong quality, so essential in learners. So when I plan lessons, I actively seek to put joy into the event." In 2000, Margaret was named Michigan Teacher of the Year and went on to be a finalist for National Teacher of the Year. She also received the Thorburn Bellringer Award, the Global Korean Award, and the United Nations Association Teacher Award. For all the accolades and for all that she gives to her students and to those in need, Margaret is an A+ educator.

Compliments to the Teacher

"When you go to her class it's a community. It's like when you're invited to someone's home. Her students will get up and greet you and make you feel welcome."

—Sherren Jones, assistant superintendent

A "Phenomenal Man": New York's Ron Clark

———————— A Defining Moment ————————

From *The Essential 55*: "Her name was Mudder . . . and she was my grandmother. As I grew up, she lived with my family and had a strong impact on who I am today. She's one of the reasons that I feel so strongly about these fifty-five expectations I have of my students, as well as all people. She, along with my parents, gave me a true southern upbringing, which included respect, manners, and an appreciation of others."

If ever Ron Clark is known more for being an author than a teacher, the general public would do well to remember all he accomplished at PS 83 in New York City. His credentials, after all, include being named Disney Teacher of the Year in 2000.

In between graduating college and stepping into the limelight, Ron traveled around Europe and even worked as a singing and dancing waiter in London, a job with obvious parallels to teaching. After eating some bad food—as the story goes, Gypsies fed him rat—he returned to North Carolina, where he happened upon a teaching job. Five years later, he was still teaching. Those five years held as much excitement as anything he'd ever done in Europe. Ron and his students were even invited to visit the White House on three occasions, but then he saw a TV show about low test scores and the lack of teachers in New York City. Next stop, Harlem, where he taught for a couple of years before the folks at Disney gave him a call.

And just like when Bill and Hillary Clinton called, Ron brought his class along to Los Angeles. They had done a bang-up job of fundraising, earning more than $25,000 to fund the trip. The same travel bug that had bitten him before Europe led him to arrange even more trips for his kids. One such trip took them to his hometown in North Carolina, where they fished, Jet-Skied, climbed rocks, and rode four-wheelers, as well as spending time at the beach. Ron's energy knows no boundaries, so it was of little surprise to family and friends when he started to turn his system of classroom management into a book. Enter the author phase of Ron's life.

He published *The Essential 55: An Award-Winning Educator's Rules for Discovering the Successful Student in Every Child* and then *The Excellent 11: Qualities Teachers and Parents Use to Motivate, Inspire, and Educate Children*. The former gained him fame and made him a *New York Times* best-selling author. The defining moment, so to speak, came when Oprah Winfrey held up his book and said, "America, you need to buy this book." He explains, "In the areas where I taught, the kids didn't have self-esteem, they didn't feel confident. I figured that if I could teach them skills, the skills would lead to confidence, and confidence would lead to pride and self-esteem. So I came up with this list of fifty-five rules that would not only teach them how to behave in school but also in life." Some of the rules include "Make eye contact," "Respect other ideas and opinions," "Say thank you within three seconds of receiving something," and "If someone bumps into you, even if it was not your fault, say 'excuse me.'"

The Essential 55 has sold over one million copies and has been published in twenty-five countries. Considering that Oprah called Ron her first "Phenomenal Man," that he has been featured on the *Today* show and CNN, and that TNT entertained nearly seven million viewers with its biopic *The Ron Clark Story*, it isn't surprising to learn that he no longer teaches at PS 83.

Despite all his personal success, it is a field trip that Ron describes when asked about his greatest moment. He says it "would have to be taking my students from North Carolina to New York City to see *Phantom of the Opera* about seven years ago . . . That performance was for them; they all felt special, and they were all lifted up." He also has gone to China to learn about its educational system, and he has taken students to Japan, Costa Rica, Russia, England, and South Africa. Now he wants to invite them to a school all his own, called the Ron Clark Academy, RCA for short.

A school for inner-city fifth- through eighth-grade students from the Atlanta area, RCA opened its doors in 2007. Ron used royalties from his books to open the nonprofit private school where tuition is $14,000 but donations offset this cost. The RCA also gives out its Great American Teacher Awards, honoring innovators in the profession.

"We are like an educational laboratory where we share what we do with teachers around the country. We have over three thousand teachers who are coming to visit us this year," he says. In talking with other educators, Ron is willing to dole out advice. "If you're going to be strict and have high expectations for your students," he explains, "then you also have to make sure they want to be in the classroom, that they enjoy being around you, they respect you, and they're having fun in there. If you are too strict, the kids will rebel. And if you try too hard to get them to like you, they're going to walk all over you. There has to be balance."

He softens up a little when he says, "I see first-year teachers come in with so much passion and want to do things different, and creatively, and they're not allowed to. Sometimes you have to fly under the radar, close your door, teach how you want to teach, but don't make too much noise about what you're doing. Then, once your kids have high test scores, then you're going to have respect, then your principal will trust you and trust what you're doing." It concerns him that so many teachers don't stick around long enough to achieve this level of trust, which is why holding on to new teachers is a priority for Ron. And he has a plan. "There are three key ways to retain good teachers at a school. (1) Don't overload them. (2) Don't give them the most difficult classes. (3) Everyone should be a mentor."

"With everything I've seen," he says, "I think I've come up with the key to successful education in America. . . . It has everything to do with teachers. I've visited some poor areas where they didn't even have an overhead projector and their scores where phenomenal because the teachers were phenomenal. They were intelligent, they were dedicated, and they had enthusiasm."

The secret of Ron's success has much to do with enthusiasm. Remembering his earliest days in the classroom, he says, "Everything I drew from came from my heart and just plain common sense. I put every hour of my life into that classroom. Even when I was sleeping— and this is God's honest truth—I would dream up lesson plans."

When he arrived in Harlem at PS 83, his first class had thirty-seven fifth-graders. That's like being plopped down amidst Genghis Khan's troops and trying to teach them about diplomacy! None of the students had met the state testing standards for fourth grade, but he made it work, saying, "I support finding innovative and creative ways to inspire kids to learn. I don't teach to the test. I teach my kids content. And I make it as fun and exciting as I can." One former student told Oprah and her audience, "Other teachers, they give up on you and say, 'You're a bad child. Who wants you? Get out of my class!' Mr. Clark, he took me for two weeks and he changed me. He brought out the inside of me and brought it right outside. Other teachers say you have to try. Mr. Clark didn't. He's the only one who believed in me. That's when I just started reaching out. He just really touched my heart, and I liked that." One thing Ron did was visit the home of each of his thirty-seven students. That goes beyond enthusiasm, but he really wanted to walk a mile in their shoes.

"One of the keys to teaching and raising children is being able to put oneself in their situation and understand their actions and emotions. If you can't relate to kids and meet them where they are, then you are going to have a tough time getting them to respect you or follow your guidance."

Another student told Oprah, "Mr. Clark gave me the strength to hold on and be somebody. That's what I'm going to be. Somebody. I'm not going to be nobody. I'm going to be somebody." Just like his teacher is somebody.

But Ron is not just "somebody," he is an A+ educator. Given that he isn't done yet, that he now has a school and a staff and a student body all his own, you have to wonder whether he can earn an even higher grade—if such an accolade even exists!

Educational Philosophy

"Do not go where the path may lead, go instead where there is no path and leave a trail."

—Ralph Waldo Emerson, quoted on the front door of the Ron Clark Academy

The Chalkboard Kid:
New Jersey's Karen Ginty

In Her Own Words

By providing a safe environment, rich with activities and infused with mutual respect and acceptance, then, and only then, will no child be left behind.

The Brookings Institution estimates that in the United States, more than six million people have teaching credentials and/or a background in teaching. Of that six million, only half are currently working in schools. This is the result of job dissatisfaction or retirement, so don't plan on adding New Jersey's Karen Ginty to that list any time soon. Despite thirty-five years of teaching, she has no plans to leave her post as a kindergarten teacher at Monmouth Beach Elementary School. And who would want her to leave? She has shown no signs of slowing down, earning the honor of New Jersey Teacher of the Year in 2007. Not bad considering she's been teaching longer than most of her students' parents have been alive.

Karen graduated from Lynchburg College in 1972 with a bachelor's degree in elementary education, then received a master's degree in early childhood education from New Jersey's Kean College. After thirty-five years of accomplishment, she takes only a moment to think of her greatest accomplishment. As Y2K came and went, Monmouth still didn't offer full-day kindergarten, as much a benefit to working parents as to their children. Karen pushed hard for full-day kindergarten, doing her research and presenting it to whoever would listen, and soon it was approved. When you consider the logistics and expense of switching from half-day to full-day kindergarten, the enormity of this achievement really comes into perspective.

When Karen was a little girl, Santa Claus brought her a brand-new chalkboard, eraser, and set of chalk. Now, thousands of people surely would like to thank Santa for Karen's gift. "I knew it was exactly what I wanted," she recalls. "I was five, loved kindergarten, and could not wait to play school at home."

Out of her parents' thoughtfulness an incredible career blossomed, and now Karen carries on their legacy of caring. "A frequent phrase we use in the classroom is 'share your kindness.' If you expect children to help each other, then they will. I often praise the children by telling them my heart is singing. . . . It always brought the best out of me when a teacher was positive and rewarding and not scolding. Kind words go further than anything negative, for all children."

"Mrs. Ginty's enthusiasm and dedication to her field are awe-inspiring," says New Jersey Commissioner of Education Lucille E. Davy. "For more than three decades, she has worked in the same school and ushered in each new school year with a fresh and friendly outlook and a love of her craft."

All that time in the same school in Monmouth and West Long Beach (where she makes her home) means that Karen has become a bit of an institution, much like her favorite musician, Bruce Springsteen. Former Mayor James P. McConville, whose two children and five nieces were taught by Karen, says, "Many times I have heard someone returning from college or visiting their parents after having moved away from town ask, 'How is Mrs. Ginty? Is she still teaching?'" For years the answer to that question has been a resounding yes.

Janet Clayton, a retired Monmouth Beach principal, shared some words that seem to say it all: "There are dedicated teachers. There are timeless teachers. There are loving and caring teachers. There are teachers with incredible integrity. There are teachers that are superb educators. Then there is Mrs. Karen Ginty. She is one of those few, special teachers who possess all of these qualities."

After winning her TOY award, Karen gave several interviews. One interviewer thought that readers might like to learn a little more about her likes and dislikes, and she was willing to share. Karen said that the three people she would most like to have dinner with are her mother, her father, and her best friend, who lives in Arizona. She said that her biggest pet peeve is dishonest people and she gave her favorite movie, *Moonstruck,* an A+. Fitting, since that is the grade the state of New Jersey gave Karen!

Educational Philosophy

Karen sums up her philosophy with the acronym SAIL. Her goal is for students to feel Safe, Accepted, and Involved so that they may Learn. "The classroom must be a nurturing and secure environment that abounds in positive feedback for all children. This ensures a sense of worthiness and self-esteem in each child.

From Ski School to High School:
Colorado's Seth Berg

In His Own Words

The mistake I made as a younger teacher was to think, "I'll help kids that are motivated; there's enough work there. If kids don't care, I won't waste time on them." But when you do that, the class splits into two warring factions who are resentful of each other. The goal is to keep everyone moving in the same boat at the same time.

Some personalities are so big, nothing can contain them. This is one of Seth Berg's gifts to the community where he lives.

Named Colorado's teacher of the year in 2007, Seth teaches math and science in Telluride. He is also the district assessment coordinator. Normally this is not a flashy job, but Seth seems to do everything with a bit of pizzazz—even assessments.

One of Seth's trademarks is that he wears a suit and tie every Friday, and after he was named teacher of the year, "the dress code at the Telluride Middle/High School was suit and tie," writes Elizabeth Guest of *Telluride Gateway.* "Still a week shy of Halloween, faculty and students flocked to class wearing their Sunday best in recognition of teacher Seth Berg."

Anyone who's ever met him understands why students and staff would be willing to dress up in Seth's honor—and that his greatest influence is Johnny Carson. Seth says, "A performer needs an audience, just as an audience needs a performance, and this relationship is equally applicable to teachers and students." He even says that he thought of Carson when developing his style of classroom management.

After majoring in science at Oberlin College, Seth became a teacher—of skiing at the Burke Mountain Academy in Vermont. He eventually earned a master's degree in education, then moved to Telluride. He quickly learned that teachers have great influence over their students, just not 100 percent influence. He likes to say, "You can lead a horse to water but you can't make him drink. It's our job as teachers to at least make him thirsty."

"Seth inspires students by building relationships and setting high, clear standards for achievement." This compliment comes from Mary Rubadeau, superintendent of schools in Telluride. Rubadeau is such a big fan of Seth's that she nominated him for teacher of the year. She has other reasons for appreciating him, too. "There's such a shortage of teachers particularly in math and science, so it is a wonderful thing for our community, but it's also great for the state to have such a thoughtful and passionate speaker representing the profession. It'll hopefully draw some younger people to the profession."

If Seth has learned one thing, it is to know the students. Not just their mother's name or what they do in their free time, but how they're feeling on a particular day. "I can tell that students are more or less open to learning depending on their emotional state. If they're too excited about a ski trip, they won't learn. Or if they're too depressed about their parents' divorce, they can't learn. If you push at the wrong time, it will backfire."

His methods and his motivations have worked, too. By his own estimation, Seth says, "I've taught, tutored, cajoled, shepherded, or threatened about five hundred local kids through successful graduations." Peter Mueller, Telluride High's principal, adds, "Seth works well with others because he focuses on how to teach students well. It's not about ego for Seth, it's about being the best educator one can be, and that is why he has established himself as a truly remarkable educator."

Seth also teaches other teachers. He often makes presentations at staff meetings, citing research to defend whatever best practice he is describing on that particular day. "Teachers are wary of 'ivory tower' advice," he says, "but they trust me because I am 'in the trenches' and my students' accomplishments confirm that I must be doing something right.

"I think the material has to be interesting and stimulating and you have to feel a sense of success and accomplishment to enjoy it. You have to respect the intellect. It is a very powerful tool, and you can figure out and research all kinds of amazing ideas. I go pretty fast. I don't like to give kids the chance to get bored or misbehave. I keep hitting them with new material, and they're pretty happy. The idea of pace works across the board. In a remedial math class, the pace might be slow and steady. But the idea of sticking to a pace and pushing ahead is consistent through all of my classes. We don't stall."

Seth is a man of many interests and has had the privilege of introducing films at each of Telluride's film festivals, Mountainfilm and Telluride Film Festival. A year-round resident, he puts more of his time into the community itself. Seth sits on the board of directors for the Pinhead Institute, a nonprofit devoted to science literacy, and One to One, a student-mentoring program. He helped build the Quest Scholarship, which grants one student per year a full ride to his or her college of choice. "We especially want to target students who are brand-new to college within their families," he says. "We'd eventually like to target fifth- and sixth-graders and get them thinking about college early."

With the honor of a teacher of the year award comes time away from the classroom. Over the course of that year, Seth traveled around the state, working with teachers on improving their craft, so for him the sabbatical was "an opportunity to send out clear advice—ideas on teacher collaboration and bonding with students in the classroom. Those are two things that can make the most difference with the least amount of money."

Seth isn't just selling a bill of goods, either. He has put tremendous time into Telluride's school reform movement, which includes weekly teacher meetings to discuss students. The goal is to make sure not one child falls through the cracks. Seth reports, "It's a way to track students on a regular basis. Sometimes kids need to be assigned to homework club, sometimes they need One to One youth services, sometimes they need scholarship help, sometimes they need tutoring options, sometimes kids might be referred to special ed, or really quick and bright students might need challenge extras."

This kind of individualized attention has been a boon to the success experienced by Telluride High School's student body. "When I first came here eighteen years ago, less than half of the graduating class went on to college," Seth remembers. "The students here were pretty resistant to the college prep approach." Now each graduating class sends 90 percent to 95 percent of its students to college. Making the extra effort to tackle all those challenges is what Seth Berg is all about. Just as he looks A+ in his suit and tie, he is indisputably an A+ educator.

A Defining Moment

"On a personal level, I'm on cloud nine," Seth said after learning he'd won the teacher of the year award. "Everyone wants to buy me champagne and flowers, but most things are the same—I'm going into the office all day tomorrow to grade papers, like I do every Sunday."

Teaching in a Virtual World:
South Dakota's Charlotte Mohling

———— *Educational Philosophy* ————

Education is a learning experience, and students may not learn on their first attempt, so they need to understand that revision and relearning may be necessary.

Gone are the days of home ec. What you will find now, in classrooms like Charlotte Mohling's, is cutting-edge technology. Stay-at-home moms, dads, or grandparents are now connected to the outside world via the Internet. "At-home" no longer has to mean isolated and out-of-touch.

Charlotte is so in tune with new technology and curriculum that she won South Dakota's teacher of the year award in 2007. She teaches family and consumer sciences and technology and has been with the Wessington Springs schools for more than thirty years. She was there back when best practice meant knowing the best recipes. She has seen her students through curricula that reflect the ethics of the times and therefore has had to constantly expand her repertoire. It's well worth it, though. Words cannot express how important today's technological advances are for kids who live far from their peers and school. On that note, Charlotte moonlights with the Dial Virtual School, which reaches out to 406 students in twenty-nine districts.

"There will be a growing need for teachers like her," says John Heemstra, director of the Dial Virtual School.

"This is rural America," Charlotte explains, "and my concern was, 'Why can't the students in my small school district have all the opportunities of students in a large school district?'" She champions remote learning through a Technology for Tomorrow lab and is able to teach students who live as far as thirty-five miles away. As is the case with any new curriculum, Charlotte had to hone her skills as a grantwriter to get the program off the ground. In total, she has written or cowritten $140,000 worth of grants to bring technology to her school, which consists of just over one hundred students.

What Charlotte has created is a modern one-room schoolhouse. In essence, it is a self-paced computer lab where she is able to facilitate fifteen Web-based courses on topics such as computer animation and desktop publishing. Her kids love it and so does she. "I truly like teaching this way. I really like making them responsible for their own learning." This control has obvious benefits for the students down the road. "I'm giving my students career options I never had, because I never had any career planning."

In addition to serving as a member of a statewide task force on personal finance, Charlotte has served as chair of the local economic development board and president of the Family and Consumer Sciences Division of the Association of Career and Technical Education. At the time of her award, she was chair of the Family and Consumer Sciences Expert Panel of the Association for Education Communications and Technology Project, and served on the National Coalition of Family and Consumer Sciences. In 2004 she was honored as a member of the All-USA Teacher Team.

Charlotte is a teacher on a mission. "I believe that my role, as a teacher, is to serve as the facilitator of that learning and not as a giver of knowledge. I want to instill in my students the desire to explore, to create, and to learn. I want to actively involve them in their education and get them excited about learning."

"I expect quality work, just as an employer would," Charlotte says. This is another hint about the changing face of family and consumer sciences and technology. Employability is also a goal. These days, what family couldn't stand to bring in a few extra dollars? In turn, Charlotte models for her kids not just work for work's sake, but finding a job you enjoy. "Going to work each day is fun! Seeing young adults achieve goals, develop positive self images, interact with peers and community members, and become actively involved in the educational process is personally rewarding and motivating."

Principal and Superintendent Darold Rounds says of Charlotte, "She has a high standard. She doesn't lower the bar just because some kid has problems." It is always impressive to observe a teacher who is both tough and nurturing. This kind of balance is needed when working with teenagers, especially those at risk of dropping out.

"One effect of the increased number of high school dropouts," she explains, "is a large group of students who are not prepared for the job market. Many of them will encounter unemployment or sporadic employment and low wages. High school dropouts may affect society as a whole. As a result of inadequate funds to support themselves or their families, they may enter the welfare system. Or they may turn to illegal methods of earning a living and end up in the prison system. This would result in increased welfare costs and growing prison populations."

Although curricula may change, not to mention the tools used to deliver them, Charlotte has developed five principles that she teaches every student. One idea is that "change is constant." She tells her students, "Don't get too comfortable with the status quo; things could, and will, change tomorrow." Her next bits of advice: "Follow your heart," as well as, "Dream, set goals, and work to achieve those goals." Next is, "Remember, life is a journey," and "on that journey you will encounter barriers, setbacks, and successes." Rather than be intimidated, she hopes her students will tackle these challenges head-on. Otherwise, the journey can be a miserable one. She continues with, "Access your allies—get to know people who can help you on your journey to success." Finally, she teaches that "learning is ongoing. Prepare yourself for the twenty-first century–continue to learn."

The image of the teacher as a magnet and the students as iron fillings works on so many levels when considering Charlotte's career and all she has accomplished. She is touching the lives of people she doesn't even see on a regular basis—she has set up a two-way video system so there can be at least some "face-to-face" contact. So many schools and their curricula are stuck in the twentieth century. For seeing the future and working to prepare her students for it, Charlotte Mohling is a cutting-edge teacher and an A+ educator.

Compliments to the Teacher

A student named Clay says, "It's all independent. You work at your own pace." Clay has taken ten of Charlotte's classes, and when he returns to the family farm from college he plans on using his advanced Web page design classes to start a Web site for the family's show cattle. Staying on-task in class is no problem, he says. "It's stuff you like to do."

Aim, Focus, Math!:
Washington, D.C.'s Jason Kamras

——————— *In His Own Words* ———————

I am often told that our nation lacks the funds to fully support public education. I reject this. The resources exist; it is the political will that is lacking. . . . We must marshal our political clout on behalf of all children.

John Philip Sousa's most famous work, "The Stars and Stripes Forever," was recorded in 1896 on one side of a seven-inch disc by the Berliner Gramophone Company; 103 years later, a math teacher cofounded a program that uses digital photography and recordable DVDs to document personal histories and the distinct neighborhoods of the nation's capital. Technology has come a long way.

The teacher is Jason Kamras and he teaches seventh- and eighth-grade math at John Philip Sousa Middle School in Washington, D.C. In 2005, six years after cofounding the EXPOSE program, Jason was named the fifty-fifth National Teacher of the Year by the Council of Chief State School Officers (CCSSO). Although photography is a passion, and new technology of great interest, Jason does not neglect his job for his hobbies. As a result of the innovative academic programs he has initiated, math scores have been on the rise at Sousa. Until recently, as many as 80 percent of the students were scoring below the basic comprehension level on their standardized tests, but now that number has been cut in half.

Given that Jason earned his bachelor's degree from Princeton University and his master's degree from Harvard University, such accomplishments as improving test scores and writing successful grants should be of no surprise. During his undergrad years, Jason cut his educational teeth by tutoring elementary-schoolers and counseling inmates interested in passing their GED, or General Educational Development, tests. He spent a summer as a VISTA (Volunteers in Service to America) volunteer, then in 1996 began his teaching career in earnest as a part of Teach for America. In less than a decade, he would be known as one of the finest teachers in the land.

"It is an honor to have a teacher like Jason in our school system because he not only serves to inspire students to academic excellence, but he can be an inspiration for his colleagues," explains Superintendent Clifford B. Janey.

"There is no lack of opportunity for Jason," says Saba Bireda, who once taught with him, "but he stays at Sousa year after year because he believes in his ability and the ability of his students to succeed despite the challenges presented to himself, his students, and the school. I can honestly say Sousa would not run effectively without Jason. Through the years he has become a de facto assistant principal, extracurricular coordinator, testing specialist, dean, and new teacher mentor. He exudes all of the qualities an excellent teacher should possess—student-specific instruction, classroom management, leadership, and above all else a devotion to see every student, regardless of school or status, reach the fullest possible potential."

On the topic of reaching potential, Jason discusses what he believes is the number-one challenge facing the nation's schools, and students, today. "We're a country of inequities, and there are many, many communities all across America where students of particular socioeconomic backgrounds are not being served adequately, quite frankly. And that has resulted in huge gaps in achievement, based on class, and race, and language of origin, and so one of my particular passions is raising awareness about these gaps and really galvanizing support for policies and mechanisms to help close these gaps. I think that one of the most important things we can do as a country is help eliminate these inequities. . . . I actually believe those inequities are the greatest social challenge facing our country today."

"Jason is very bright, energetic, and forward-looking," says Jon Quam, director of the National Teacher of the Year program. "He has committed himself to schools with difficulty in attracting large numbers of high-qualified professionals and to under-resourced schools."

The pace of the turnover rate increases each year as more and more baby boomers retire, especially in underfunded inner-city schools. As new teachers enter the field, mentors must help them learn the tricks of the trade, and Jason gladly steps into this role. He says, "One of the things I suggest to new teachers as they enter the classroom is to demonstrate that they're really serious about the business of learning, and about setting a high standard for the students and the classroom. That immediately sets a tone of 'we're really going to achieve this year.' Children actually want that. They're thirsting for that push, for that order, for that notion that someone is going to lead them in a very systematic way. But then there are also all sorts of other things you can do—spending time with children outside the classroom, going to chess tournaments and basketball games, making home visits, getting to know the families—so that you do develop a sense of rapport and trust that you can then draw upon in the classroom."

Though some might pale at the idea of home visits, the fact that they help in building relationships and in being able to maintain order in the classroom, is undeniable. On top of that, Jason says, "The best classroom-management system is a great, engaging lesson. Take the time to plan carefully so that your students will enter your classroom every day wondering, 'What exciting surprises does s/he have in store for me today?'" Still, he can't help but come back to the idea of high expectations, saying, "Set clear (and high!) expectations for your students. Let them know what you expect them to learn and how you expect them to treat each other. Once you set the bar high, children inevitably rise to the occasion." And Jason knows the best way to go about tailoring instruction to meet the needs of individual students: "Effective differentiation is absolutely critical in all classrooms. It's also one of the most challenging (and rewarding!) parts of teaching.

Our students have incredibly diverse learning needs. It's our obligation to ensure that we're meeting every single one."

This is both an obligation and a challenge, and one that Jason meets head-on every day. "Teaching is very demanding work, very difficult, but the opportunity to work with my children is one I cherish every day. They are incredibly bright, incredibly dynamic, and creative, and resilient. There's honestly no group of people I'd rather get up in the morning to see every day."

Jason is still a young man. Walk into his classroom and you might mistake him for a rookie teacher, but he is a veteran—and a well-decorated one at that. So what does the future hold for him? "Perhaps one day down the line I'd like to open up my own school and try my hand at broadening my impact, and see if I can be successful as a school leader, in addition to being a teacher."

At Sousa, Jason Kamras is working hard to keep alive the idea of America as the land of opportunity. You can almost hear him humming a Sousa march as he makes his way to school in the morning, ready for another day of proving that he is an A+ educator. The more he broadens his impact, the better.

— Advice for Teachers New and Experienced —
Don't forget to emphasize the positive. There's great power in highlighting the positive behaviors and positive efforts of students.

"The Atoms Family Started . . .":
Hawaii's Pascale Creek Pinner

In Her Own Words

Without teachers, children could not grow up to be inventors, doctors, lawyers, gardeners, or any other passion that they so choose. Seeing the paths that different children may select and then leading them gently in a direction that you know will fulfill their potential is one of the largest responsibilities of a teacher.

One of the stories about Pascale Creek Pinner is that she likes to alter the lyrics to *The Addams Family* when introducing the atoms unit to her students. At first glance, this might seem like an easy, obvious move, but her students didn't see it that way then and they don't see it that way now. Eighth-graders are usually an energetically cynical group, but Pascale's students genuinely like the song. They learn it and end up singing right along with "The Atoms Family." This is what good teachers do: get their students on board and then together they sing.

"You have to vary how you teach things to kids," Pascale says. "You need to have that ability to stand up, move around, sing, dance. That's important."

Pascale teaches earth/space science classes at Hilo Intermediate School in Hilo, Hawaii. She also has a Gifted and Talented class. After twenty-one years of teaching, she is convinced that hers is the most important career anyone can have. "Teachers are the providers of truth and opportunity."

In 2008 the truth of Pascale's talent became big news when she was named Hawaii's teacher of the year. Her colleagues and administrators couldn't have been happier. "The teacher of the year award is one of our premier events to say thank you for the hard work that they do," says Superintendent Pat Hamamoto, beaming. "It's not only inspiring, it gives all of us hope that our teachers are doing what we know they can do best, and that is to take care of our children and give them the skills for the twenty-first century." And what about Pascale, in particular? Hamamato notes that her classroom is a "place of innovation," emphasizing problem-solving, creativity, and higher-order thinking skills.

Pascale has also been recognized on the national level. She earned her certification from the National Board for Professional Teaching Standards and received a Presidential Award for Excellence, the nation's highest honor for educators certified in math and science. She is also on the Teacher Advisory Council to the National Academy of Science. With these recognitions comes responsibility, and Pascale is up to the task. "Being a great teacher means that you share your knowledge with others and learn from as many experiences as you can so that you can continue to be a lifelong learner yourself."

When sharing knowledge with new teachers, she likes to say, "Stick to it! Persevere and you will see the benefits of teaching come to pass. The beginning years are traumatic but as you get your 'bag of tricks' together, you will see the joy of learning reflected in your student's eyes and you will know that you are truly a teacher! Remember, life is not a dress rehearsal; we get one time through, and using our life to the benefit of others, as well as growing as a person, is really what being a teacher is all about."

Pascale's principal sees what drives her star teacher. "She has a belief in kids that they will," says Elaine Christian, "that they can."

Pascale's belief in her kids is sometimes at odds with the beliefs of the school. Of one such memory, she writes, "I knew that I had broken a school rule about not turning Justin in for having a cigarette, but I just knew in my heart that punishment was not what was needed and that my decision that day could be the 'make or break' difference that this child needed—someone to care and talk to, instead of someone to punish, which is all he really ever knew." Several years later, while waiting at the airport, she ran into Justin and he said, "I just wanted to tell you how much your care and concern for me in eighth grade meant to me over the last few years." As an adult, Justin is now working to help abused children.

"A great teacher is one who always cares that their children learn," Pascale states, "even when challenged with those who just don't want to for various reasons. . . . Teaching is a demanding career that takes a heart filled with hope and translates that into action for every child in a community."

Hilo Intermediate is a community, too, one in which Pascale fits perfectly. In addition to her wonderful teaching, she is involved in the young astronaut program and has written several grants. She also teaches curriculum to her fellow teachers. A colleague says, "We demand a lot of our kids—not just in learning but in social skills and community service. Because Pascale has set high expectations for the kids, they want to meet them as much as possible. . . . [The teacher of the year award] not only recognizes Pascale for her awesome work but also them. They appreciate seeing a teacher they have such great respect for being honored for trying to provide them a first-class education against all odds."

Pascale's belief in her students, not to mention the faith she has in her fellow teachers, is one reason she has been recognized as a model teacher. When you picture her singing "The Atoms Family," reaching out to a student in need after school, and writing grants to fund integral programs, it isn't hard to believe that Pascale Creek Pinner is considered an A+ educator.

Compliments to the Teacher

"We would not have technology in the school without her," says Principal Elaine Christian. "Science Fair would not happen without her. She's an awesome lady. She works constantly. She comes [to the teacher of the year ceremony] and she's correcting papers!"

A Curator in Teacher's Clothing:
Kansas's Keil E. Hileman

—————— *Educational Philosophy* ——————

The leaps and bounds that our educational system has made in the last one hundred years are very small compared to what we will have to do in the next one hundred years. There is a tidal wave of information and technological change coming that most Americans are unaware of.

Monticello Trails Middle School teacher Keil Hileman is a man of action—selfless, purposeful action. Not only does Keil coach girls' volleyball, basketball, and track, he works with students to restore all of Monticello's old trophies, some of which date back to the 1920s. This is because Keil, a social studies teacher, understands the value of artifacts. For him, there is no better learning tool.

"I believe it is the teacher's responsibility to determine what it will take to enable students to explore the world they live in, empower them with useful learning, and excel by applying that knowledge to achieve educational and personal goals in their everyday lives." In using artifacts to help his students explore their world, a world they have inherited from others, Keil has created something bigger than him and his students—so big, in fact, that it is even bigger than his classroom.

What Keil and his students have created is the Classroom Museum. Now housed in a room twice the size of his own, the museum is the first housed by a public school. Keil's artifact collection stands at approximately ten thousand items, and he knows whom he has to thank. "The parents, individually and through my partnership with PTO [Parent Teacher Organization], have been incredibly supportive, and they have never denied a museum request." A more personal story shows how this museum got its start.

Keil began bringing in his own personal artifacts to help beef up his lessons. Then he started asking students to bring artifacts of their own from home. A student named Jason gave Keil a note from his grandmother. It read, "If you promise to never sell them and always use them to teach, they are yours to keep." What those artifacts were, no one can remember, but it was a watershed moment in Keil's career and it put Monticello on the map.

Among the artifacts in Keil's collection are a slave collar from the 1790s, a 1796 flintlock musket, an 1898 brass cash register, a porcelain barber chair from the 1920s, a 1907 nickel and cast-iron stove, and a Chinese coin that is three thousand years old. Keil lends his artifacts to other teachers as part of his Creating a Museum in Your Room program. But fellow teachers aren't the only ones interested in using the artifacts.

"Many former students check out artifacts to take to their high school and college classes," Keil says proudly. "The unique and creative tool I use to motivate and teach my students has now become a permanent entity that will last beyond me. The museum is not only a place of learning for me and my students, it has become our community's museum." In addition to his regular duties, Keil now gets the chance to work with all of his school's students through his Museum Connections curriculum. He helps the other Monticello social studies teachers use this model to teach history, and he says, "This will increase my annual number of students from 100 to 550."

Keil has presented at the annual conference of the National Council of Social Studies in Orlando, Florida, and for Project Whistle Stop. He received a De Soto Foundation Grant in 2000 and used the money to buy dolls from around the world, which he uses to teach about other cultures and customs.

The year 2004 marked Keil's tenth year in the classroom, as well as the year he was named Kansas's teacher of the year. In addition, he was a finalist for National Teacher of the Year, and three years before, he was nominated for Disney Teacher of the Year.

In addition to coaching several sports, and despite being a social studies teacher, Keil is the school's math team coach. At the time of his award, he had mentored eight teachers. He is an Eagle Scout and teaches archaeology classes for students in grades five through nine as part of the Johnson County Community College Summer Talents Program. Keil volunteers for food drives that benefit local folks as well as people in Sudan, gives his time and effort to Toys for Tots every year, and makes sure to create opportunities for his students to act on behalf of others as well.

"Mr. Hileman has taken a subject that he cares deeply about and changed other people's minds so that they, too, have become passionate about it," says Jamie, a former student. "He knew what would touch us, what would change us, and used that to make us learn."

"My job is to teach," Keil says, "but my passion is setting students' minds ablaze with a love of creative learning and the power of knowledge." He adds, "I am a teacher who keeps them on their toes and occasionally surprises them. They rarely know what new adventure awaits them in my class each day."

In addition to the surprises, there is the need to address the individual needs of each student, which Keil accomplishes through differentiated instruction. "The challenges I place before my students help them grow socially, academically, and intellectually. I use multilevel or tiered assignments, which allow students to achieve success at many different levels. While some students only complete the initial level of the assignment, other students' abilities allow them to go much farther and accomplish more."

Going farther seems to be something Keil has mastered. As if sharing his artifacts and his museum curriculum isn't enough, he has used his knowledge of technology to help teachers incorporate Power-Point presentation software into their curriculum. This enables them to display information for students and to print notes and outlines for students who are absent or have "notes provided" as a part of their individualized education plan.

The work with his students, though, remains at the heart of what Keil does so well on a daily basis. And the museum itself is a testament to this, an artifact of learning in its own right. Of his museum activities, Keil says the value is clear. His lessons are built around "higher-level thinking skills and problem-solving activities linked to real historical events." The long-term benefit is that "students take these learning achievements and build upon them to change who they are as people. These achievements enable them to excel for the rest of their lives. This constantly ignites a commitment and dedication in me that pushes me to excel in all that I do in regard to teaching my students. I enjoy making social studies and world history come alive for my students."

Others have excitedly recognized just how good Keil is at bringing history to life. In the letter of recommendation, colleagues on his seventh-grade Trailblazers teaching team wrote, "His enthusiasm is never-ending; his creativity is astounding; his compassion for his students is inspiring; his love and passion for his subject area is overwhelming."

For creating a teaching tool that will impact thousands of students and teachers, Keil has been recognized across the nation as a fantastic teacher. Because he has been able to bring history to life for so many people, Keil deserves a place among the A+ educators.

—— *Advice for Teachers New and Experienced* ——
Become a risk-taker. Go out on a limb. Often the limb you step out on will act as a catapult and take you and your students to wonderful places you never imagined existed.

Ain't No Climbing Wall High Enough:
Oregon's Michael Geisen

"I think if he wanted to, he could make watching grass grow interesting." This compliment comes from Karlie, one of Michael Geisen's former students, and that just about says it all.

But can he make students have fun during a test?

"I try to put a bit of myself, a bit of Prineville, and a good dose of humor and creativity into each activity, project, or assignment," says Michael, a seventh-grade science teacher at Crook County Middle School in Prineville, Oregon. "In fact, students even laugh during tests in our class." You might be inclined to chalk this up to hyperbole and exaggeration, but after Karlie's comment, the claim is indisputable. Besides, Michael has one heckuva resume, at the top of which is the 2008 National Teacher of the Year award. Not too shabby for a guy who was once lost in the woods.

Michael's undergraduate degree is in forest resource management, and while working at the University of Washington he began to take the road less traveled. "For twelve to fourteen hours a day, I designed and implemented exercises to teach forestry majors the field skills they needed to succeed, and spent hours in the forest helping them, guiding them, and getting to know them. But for several years I had been working as a professional forester using those same skills . . . alone. One day on a rainy hillside, I realized why I was barely able to get up every morning: I needed to give. My vocation needed to have deeper meaning, to have relationship, to have heart. I needed to teach." So he went back to school and eventually went to work *at* a school.

One unit, in particular, effectively illustrates why Michael won the National Teacher of the Year award. "This award was given in recognition of the hundreds of volunteer hours I spent fund-raising, planning, and constructing a 1,000-square-foot rock-climbing wall at our school. I also secured donations of gear from dozens of companies, designed an integrated curriculum, and taught several elective climbing courses over the years, which were immensely popular with students."

Michael loves teaching so much that his colleagues like to tell the tale of the day he totaled his car on the way to CCMS but still made it to school.

"I allow my curiosity and enthusiasm for learning to match my students'," Michael says, "and we inspire each other to further explore and wonder about the big questions and the little details that make our world so fascinating." He admits, though, that it took him awhile to find his stride in the classroom. "When I first began my teaching career, I saw myself as a teacher of *science*. I quickly realized that middle school teachers are actually teachers of *students* and that the subject matter was somewhat secondary. I am now starting to realize that our true job is actually teacher of the *community*."

To help build a sense of community with his students, he worked with a colleague named Tawnya Layne to develop a celebration called "The Night of the Electric Creation," where families come to the school to eat dinner together and see the projects their children have created. Then there are his charitable acts. Michael's community service projects are local (recycling programs through the U.S. Forest Service) and global (the 3rd World Hunger Relief Club), and he involves his students as often as he can. That said, it is the art of relationship-building that Michael tries to share with other teachers. "If we are going to unite students together into a community of learners," he advises, "each classroom needs to be warm, welcoming, and inviting to everyone. I make it a goal to greet students each day as they enter, call them by name as often as possible, and to use humor to break down barriers of class, race, age, and ability."

Then it's time to hit them with science. "When students are interested, they start to ask real questions. And when they ask questions, they're on their way to becoming great scientists and learners. This enthusiasm becomes contagious, and kids spread it around our building and take it home to their families. It doesn't happen every day for every child, but it happens frequently enough to call it a pattern." One example of enthusiasm starting with Michael and spreading to students and fellow science teachers is the courtyard outside the school's science wing. Together, they created "an outdoor learning laboratory that was both beautiful and a scientifically accurate model of the native vegetation zones from the Oregon coast to the high desert." With support from a variety of sources, Michael says, "we transformed the courtyard into a place of beauty and pride, complete with trees, shrubs, native grasses, walkways, benches, topography, and a drip irrigation system. This year we have begun work on two water features that will mimic runoff from the Cascade Mountains, and are about to lay sod to provide a grassy teaching area." There are opportunities for future efforts, too. For example, students plan to paint a mural of local flora and fauna. "The outdoor learning lab will be used for years to come to teach numerous science topics, provide a quiet reading and study area, and to daily lift the spirits of students and staff at our school."

In addition to such multidisciplinary efforts, Michael contributes to the school by overseeing assessment—no small task these days. He does it because he knows what an effective teaching tool data can be. "As benchmark coordinator for the middle school science department, I lead the six-person science team in its quest to root out the iniquities of scientific illiteracy. In the past several years our strategies, commitment, and enthusiasm have led to an increase in our state test scores from 44 percent (meets or exceeds) to 72 percent." Despite his position, Michael feels that today's students are being put at risk with too much testing. He also says excessive testing takes a lot of control and creativity out of the teacher's hands. He could live with this if he thought it would really help teachers with all the different kinds of kids they work with.

Like any good teacher, Michael views closing the achievement gap as a priority. It is less clear what percentage of teachers support, as he does, homogeneous grouping in the classroom. This is the practice of putting together students of similar skill and background knowledge when deciding on class schedules, and Michael sees this method— called "tracking" in some districts—as the best means of meeting the needs of diverse learners. He thinks it is the best way to close the gaps and that plenty of data support this.

In everything he does, Michael puts his students first, including serving on such committees as the district leadership team. He says, "We have brainstormed, developed, and begun implementation of a district-wide technology program. This school year our program includes a laptop in the hands of every sixth-grader in the district, adding another grade each year!" The last thing Michael needs is another meeting to attend, but technology helps his students reach new heights of achievement, so attend he does.

In a time when high-quality science teachers are hard to come by, it's nice to know great teachers are out there ready and willing to mentor the newly certified first-timers. It's nice to know there are A+ educators like Michael Geisen getting his students ready for high school, college, and the world.

Educational Philosophy

In my teaching I strive to bring together creativity and science, to unite my students into a community, and to help each person in this community connect with the big ideas of science.

Mastering the Middle School Mind: Wisconsin's Beth A. Oswald

In middle school, students are living in two worlds. Although the urge to grow up, act like a grown-up, and be treated like a grown-up is threaded through much of what they do and say, there are still palpable signs of the child inside. Half elementary schooler, half high schooler, kids in middle school have a hard time making sense of their world. Sixth-graders are still pretty innocent, but, as the saying goes, once kids hit seventh- and eighth-grade, they start "smelling themselves." They get some swagger and some sass. They show off a little and they test a little more to figure out what they can get away with and who they want to be. But the only thing harder than being a middle schooler is teaching middle schoolers.

So you use rubber chickens. You throw toga parties. You get everyone to be medieval for the day. You treat the kids like teenagers some of the time and at other times you invite the families in to celebrate their work so the kids feel that sense of accomplishment while basking in innocent childhood joy. Social studies teacher Beth Oswald knows how to walk this line for her students, teaching to both halves of their bodies and brains. Middle school teachers are a special breed, and she is the model for them.

As a seasoned teacher of seventh- and eighth-graders, Beth keeps an assortment of rubber chickens in a box behind her desk. They are her version of the conch shell from *Lord of the Flies*. Whoever holds the rubber chicken has the floor. Conversely, it's a reward. If you speak, you get to hold the rubber chicken. And "everybody wants to hold on to the rubber chicken," Beth says. "They absolutely must hold on to the rubber chicken. Even the quietest kid will generally come out of their shell for the rubber chicken." With this cool trick, Beth is able to promote class participation, even after her students have moved out of that please-the-teacher, elementary school stage.

She says, "I try and keep them doing stuff. I get them out of their seat at least once during the class if I can."

Each year Beth turned her annual Egypt project into a student-created Museum of Ancient Civilizations. The students designed labels for the exhibits, organized the exhibits, served as curators, and gave tours to other students, parents, and teachers. Beth sees the work leading up to the creation of the museum, and the museum itself, as a means of teaching the curriculum as well as teaching essential skills. "My main goal is if they can learn something about history but also learn how to be a good group member, be a good participant, be a good listener. All those things are going to take them further in life than knowing the years that King Tut ruled."

Fellow teacher RuthAnn Yoerger describes the joy the kids experience once the museum is complete and the public turns out to see what they have done. "It is awesome to see the pride on students' faces!"

Principal Robert Flaherty likes to attend Beth's celebrations, including the Museum of Ancient Civilizations, Toga Day, and Medieval Day. Flaherty is so impressed with her teaching, he nominated Beth for a Kohl Fellowship. In 2007 she was named one of eighty-six Kohl Fellows and then, out of that talented pool, she earned statewide recognition as Wisconsin's 2008 teacher of the year. Beth teaches at J. C. McKenna Middle School and had been there for eleven years when she was nominated. In addition to her top-notch teaching, she is an award-winning student council adviser. Her student-government leaders have organized fund-raisers for Kosovo, 9/11, Hurricane Katrina, and the March of Dimes.

Beth has also been active promoting certain causes with Wisconsin's government. She has advocated for extending family leave time and spoke before the Senate Education Committee about the importance of the parent-teacher relationship. "I can really, truly say the more you develop a face-to-face relationship with a parent, the more likely that parent is going to feel comfortable initiating contact again with you," she says. "These parents are also much more likely to respond in a positive manner when contacted regarding any concerns staff may have about their child, as they now see teachers as partners, rather than adversaries. Additionally, once parent-teacher relationships are formed through contact at open houses and conferences, parents tend to feel more comfortable attending school-day activities."

Opening the class museum up to the public is one way of building these kinds of relationships. Helping parents understand that the changes their seventh-graders are experiencing are typical is another. Beth manages to partner with the students just as she partners with their parents. She succeeds in her balancing act much as her students succeed in theirs, living in the past while also preparing for their future. For her empathy and her creativity, Beth is an A+ educator.

In Her Own Words

I love to let them create meaning for themselves, let them talk. They want to be heard. You can see that. They want to be able to share their stories. They want to be able to share their ideas.

Be the Person You Want the Children to Be:
California's Rafe Esquith

In His Own Words

Rafe says, "I became a teacher because my father taught me that a life without service is a wasted life." The roots of Rafe's service go back to his father's passing when Rafe was just nine years old. "I know what it's like to grow up without a mentor. I know what a difference an extra person in a life can make."

In a book full of fantastic teachers, perhaps none is more qualified for inclusion, none more famous, than Hobart Boulevard Elementary School's Rafe Esquith. Hobart, located in Los Angeles, is the second largest elementary school in the United States. More than 90 percent of its students live below the poverty line and most come from Central American and Korean families, which means that a majority of Rafe's fifth-graders are learning English as a second language.

Of all the great things Rafe has done and continues to do, what stands out is the way he teaches about William Shakespeare. Every year, his students perform one of his plays, and occasionally they even take the show on the road. The class has performed with the Royal Shakespeare Company and has appeared at the Globe Theater in London. PBS even aired a documentary, *The Hobart Shakespeareans,* which highlighted the year Esquith's class spent learning and performing *Hamlet.* Even the in-class performances are special. Janet, a former student, says, "I wish I could put all the feelings from that evening into a jar and carry it around with me wherever I go, because the emotions in Room 56 that night were full of delight, passion, and energy. Putting together those plays every year not only taught me about Shakespeare, but about teamwork and humility, and that when one of my fellow classmates was onstage, it was his turn to be in the spotlight, not mine."

After a few years of national recognition for his thespians, there were plenty of invitations to move out of the classroom and into the world of professional development. Rafe politely declined. To be a teacher or not to be? There was no question in Rafe's mind.

"Esquith's methods," reports National Public Radio's Michele Norris, "have been so successful that he has been encouraged to leave the classroom to help other instructors. But he has no interest in abandoning his kids." "Well," Rafe says, "we always say, 'no child left behind.' I see a lot of teachers now who win an award or two, and they write their book and they get their Web site, and then they leave. Talk about no child left behind, they leave them all behind! I can't do that."

Instead of leaving his students behind, Rafe carries on with his teaching, his love of the kids, and his love of literacy. He is a writer and his book, *Teach Like Your Hair's on Fire: The Methods and Madness Inside Room 56*, is intended to help other urban educators. Remembering a student who had trouble starting her chemistry experiment, Rafe explains how the book got its name: "In trying to get her alcohol burner to light, I set my hair on fire and didn't even know it until the kids started screaming. But as ridiculous as that was, I actually thought, if I could care so much I didn't even know my hair was on fire, I was moving in the right direction as a teacher—when I realized that you have to ignore all the crap, and the children are the only thing that matter."

The secret of his success has always been the amount of time he puts into not only his students, but also into working *with* his students, many of whom come in two hours before the school day starts, work with him rather than go out to recess, and then stay after school until it's time to go home for dinner. Somehow, Rafe has also found the time to coach the school's math team, which once had a five-year undefeated streak. As if this weren't enough, he also runs the Young Authors project, which results in each student producing a book. Whatever he does with the kids, Rafe serves as a role model. "I want my kids to work hard, so I've got to be the hardest worker they've ever seen," he says. This theory also works in teaching social skills. "I don't raise my voice to these kids; I don't humiliate these children. I'm a tough teacher, but if I want them to be nice to each other, I better be the nicest guy they ever met."

A lot of folks find Rafe to be among the nicest and most talented people they have ever met. This includes the media. The *Washington Post* described Rafe as "the most interesting and influential classroom teacher in the country." The *New York Times* reported that "Rafe Esquith is a genius and a saint." *Newsday* called Rafe "a modern-day Thoreau, preaching the value of good work, honest self-reflection and the courage to go one's own way." And *Time* noted that "politicians, burbling over how to educate the underclass, would do well to stop by Rafe Esquith's fifth-grade class."

"While my wife believes me to be eccentric," Rafe says, "good friends of mine have not been so gentle, going as far as to label me quixotic at best and certifiable at worst." He laughs, "I teach with 125 teachers. Most of them are incredibly nice to me, and eight or ten believe I'm the Antichrist. And that's OK. The best teacher who ever lived was Socrates and they killed him."

Rafe's common-sense attitude is evident in the classroom where he uses play money, paying his students salaries for their hard work and fining them when they don't do their homework. At $50 a fine, the homework gets done! And Rafe's classroom is intended to replicate, as closely as possible, the real world. That's why his walls are decorated with college banners. They are reminders of a greater world and are a tribute to the schools his former students have attended. These colleges and universities really do exist and you really can attend one if you set your mind to it—that's the message Rafe is sending. "The real measure of a teacher is not that the kids like him or that they do well at the tests at the end of the year. The real measure is where are these children five years from now, ten years from now? What am I giving to these children that they'll be using for the rest of their lives?" In addition to the college banners, there are classroom mottos. One reads, "Be nice. Work hard." A second reads, "There are no shortcuts."

As in any classroom, it's a reciprocal relationship. Both sides ask a lot, and both sides give a lot. Everyone benefits. "The kids are proud of the trust I give them, and they do not want to lose it. They rarely do, and I make sure on a daily basis that I deserve the trust I ask of them." The students would be hard-pressed to find a teacher who deserves their trust more, and that's why Rafe Esquith is an A+ educator.

A Defining Moment

In 1992 Rafe was named Disney's National Outstanding Teacher of the Year. In addition, he won Oprah Winfrey's $100,000 Use Your Life Award, a Sigma Beta Delta Fellowship from Johns Hopkins University, *Parents Magazine's* As You Grow Award, the president's National Medal of Arts, and the Dalai Lama Compassion in Action Award. Finally, and perhaps most impressive, he was made an honorary Member of the Order of the British Empire by Queen Elizabeth!

A Renaissance Woman:
Iowa's Vicki Lynn Goldsmith

—————————— *In Her Own Words* ——————————

The arts have the power to help students develop as whole, imaginative, healthy human beings. The emotional connections that emerge in the arts are more important than spitting back facts or plugging in the right answer, because making something with our own bodies has to be a valid creation since it represents our own feelings. Students who are engaged and invested in what they're doing find their own voices.

Roosevelt High School's Vicki Lynn Goldsmith is not your typical teacher. In addition to teaching English, she handles women's studies and theories of knowledge, elective classes that sound more like what one might find in college rather than high school. Students in her women's studies class might want to contemplate what the counterpart to the phrase "Renaissance man" might be. When they reach consensus, that nickname could certainly be applied to Vicki.

A teacher since 1962, Vicki has taught in seven secondary schools and six colleges and universities. Three of those college-level jobs were in Poland and Taiwan. While in Taiwan she was a student at a Chinese cooking school and ended up editing two Chinese cookbooks. On her résumé is a teaching stint at an Air Force base, one at an Army post (she worked with Native American students and the children of sheep ranchers), and one in a prison. Vicki is a huge supporter of the arts and received a National Endowment for the Humanities grant for work on Greek mythology. She has been at Des Moines's Roosevelt High School since 1989.

In 2005 the well-rounded Vicki was named Iowa's teacher of the year. When her application was reviewed by the folks in Washington,

D.C., she was selected as a finalist for National Teacher of the Year. It isn't surprising to learn that Vicki had no complaints about not winning. She prefers to take things in stride and not feed in to the angst and rush of the modern world.

"Our culture is racing at a pace that is discouraging focus and attention on huge questions," she says. "The media presents an overstimulating, oversexualized, hyped message that sabotages our efforts to get young people to examine what is worth being and doing." For Vicki, teaching is worth doing, and a reflective, pensive person is worth being. For example, she offers a solution to this "racing at a pace" problem: "We need to face the issue in classes, look at the multitasking we do, examine the motives of politicians and advertisers, spend at least some time daily being quiet and alone. We need to ask whether a new development in technology, for instance, is a real improvement in the quality of our lives or just a change."

Listening to her discuss these matters, you can easily imagine how stimulating the debates in her classroom are. Vicki is in tune with the arts and with current events. She clearly understands human nature and change and hopes to keep both moving in a positive direction.

Regarding the overstimulation of children, she says, "It is important to examine our culture and watch how the changes in society are manifested in the classroom. Our daily pace, with its channel-surfing and multitasking, makes reading seem slow. We become addicted to that speed and have trouble sustaining focus and digging deeply into a subject. Students need to learn to experience solitude and to sit in discomfort to examine the source of an idea."

In terms of how the art of teaching fits into this fast-paced society, Vicki admits, "Teaching is more difficult than it has ever been. If our education system is to encourage the critical thinking necessary for a dynamic democracy, if we are to help all students reach their highest human potential, if we are to envision education as the means of transforming lives, now more than ever, we must draw the best minds and hearts into teaching and make education competitive with other professions."

Ever the optimist, though, she says, "I believe that education should go beyond facts and information or job training and transform a human being, enabling him or her to live a richer, fuller life, to understand the connection between us and our world."

What is the common-sense secret to her success? She says, "I use as much experiential activity as possible to engage students in learning with their minds, bodies, and imaginations. They need to know how to relate to and listen to each other, how to tolerate and respect others' beliefs, so we spend a lot of time listening to each other."

Summing it all up, this A+ educator does as all A+ educators do: she provides food for thought. "The media tell us we never need to be in pain and that we can escape through pills, food, drugs, or entertainment. It is important that we teach young people how to sit through the discomfort necessary to feel the present moment fully and to stay with a disturbing new idea to examine its source. The pace of our lives and the emphasis on efficiency and multitasking discourage real grappling with issues. We can counteract the detachment caused by acceleration, violence, and technology in our society by building into our curricula those exercises that strengthen community and allow us to know ourselves and others. We must connect to address such social issues as our fear of our own multiculturalism. If we want graduates to think of art, literature, and history as ways to solve problems, we must examine what is worth knowing, doing, and becoming."

--- *Advice for Teachers New and Experienced* ---

Pay attention to each student one at a time, and keep your passion for your subject.

Avoiding Prison and Surviving a Hurricane:
Louisiana's Laurie R. Carlton

In Her Own Words

I think Louisiana is a very progressive state with our education, very innovative. But we really need to promote ourselves more. We need to bring dignity back and realize we're doing the most noble of professions.

A veteran teacher, Laurie Carlton has been honing her craft for fourteen years. Still, she vividly remembers the time she spent, way back when, as a teacher in a rehabilitation program for inmates at the Orleans Parish Prison. Her students were all males, ages sixteen to sixty-five. Like with most classes, she remembers the broad range of aptitudes and educational backgrounds. Some could barely read or write, but "one inmate told me, had he done this well in school, he probably wouldn't have gotten in trouble and gone to jail." She smiles. "The way the story went, I just started teaching right."

Laurie will never forget those she has to thank for reigniting her desire to teach and helping her to finally find her calling. "It was the inmates that encouraged me to go back into the classroom."

The story gets even more interesting: before her time with those unlikely students, Laurie had walked away from a completely normal, traditional teaching position. After just one year at Edna Karr Junior High School, she'd quit. "I thought they [the students] were the problem because they didn't get their lessons or because of their discipline problems. After I left I realized I was the problem."

That experience, coupled with the time at Orleans Parish Prison, taught Laurie a lot about the people in her charge. "I learned to meet the individual needs of students. I know now I really need to evaluate the levels of the people I teach."

Fast-forward to 2008 and the announcement of the Louisiana Teacher of the Year. Almost two years to the day after Hurricane Katrina made landfall, spirits were high in the room as all in attendance appreciated having something to celebrate. In part, the ceremony was a thank-you to those teachers who had stayed after so many fled.

"As I have toured the state," announced State Superintendent of Education Paul G. Pastorek, "I have heard from educators across Louisiana who assure me that there are many terrific teachers who work with our children. These outstanding teachers that we recognize today prove the point." Then Pastorek brought Laurie up to the stage as *the* outstanding teacher.

Senator Mary L. Landrieu added, "Laurie Carlton is a beacon of hope in an area still recovering from Hurricane Katrina. She is an incredible classroom leader and goes above and beyond with her involvement in the community."

And to think she had come so close to leaving the classroom permanently . . .

The award came as a result of the good work Laurie is doing with her ninth- and twelfth-grade students at Belle Chasse High School. She teaches English I, English I Honors, and English IV, is a member of the Louisiana Comprehensive Curriculum Assessment Development Committee, and is a mentor to fellow teachers, volunteers in the district attorney's office, and helps run a program at the American Legion that gives Christmas presents to abused children. She is pursuing a master's degree in educational leadership and recently became a National Board Certified Teacher.

"English was not one of my best classes," says Brad, a former student, "but she made it fun. It was my last class of the day and it was a class I looked forward to."

Laurie also has the support and respect of her principal, Monica Wertz. "She really, really works hard to build good relationships with all students, whether she teaches them or not."

It isn't a stretch to think that, somewhere in Louisiana, an adult is sleeping in a bed rather than a cell bunk because of Laurie's teaching. It isn't a stretch to think that because of teachers like Laurie, Louisiana schools will survive the destruction of Hurricane Katrina. For all she has done and all she will do, Laurie Carlton is an A+ educator.

A Defining Moment

Under the Restart Program, the U.S. Department of Education made initial payments of $100 million to Louisiana, $100 million to Mississippi, $50 million to Texas, and $3.75 million to Alabama to help schools recover from Hurricane Katrina and Hurricane Rita. One year after Katrina, only 33 percent of schools in Orleans Parish, as well as Plaquemines and St. Bernard Parishes, had reopened.

From GED to University Library:
Michigan's Thomas A. Fleming

—— *Advice for Teachers New and Experienced* ——

Remember, the future of every young man or woman you meet is not your responsibility alone. You will play your part, and what you teach, day by day, semester by semester, with all the clarity and passion you can summon, will contribute to, but not determine, the outcome of their lives. You may not see the results at the time. Nevertheless, your contribution is significant.

Is it possible for a high school dropout to earn the honor of National Teacher of the Year? You betcha!

In 1991 Thomas Fleming was pleased to learn that he had been named Michigan's teacher of the year. Special education teachers are humble by nature and tend to take their victories in small doses, be it Adequate Yearly Progress or just being witness to a child with dyslexia spelling his or her own name. So it must have been quite a shock when a school year that began with a statewide honor ended in national recognition.

Not only does Tom, now known as Dr. Fleming, teach special education, he teaches it at the Washtenaw County Juvenile Detention Center in Ann Arbor. For much of his career, he has taught integrated history, government, and geography to twelve- to sixteen-year-olds in a one-room-schoolhouse type of setting. The students hold a special place in Tom's heart because they remind him of a teenage boy who dropped out of high school and joined the National Guard many years ago. That boy was Tom, and after four years of service in the Guard and two more years in the Army, he earned his General Education Development diploma by going to night school. After his bachelor's degree, Tom attended Eastern Michigan University (EMU) for his master's degree. Long gone were thoughts of dropping out. Now Tom was tuned in to his life's mission: teaching.

And teach he did. Tom taught emotionally disturbed students at two state hospitals and then those kids at the juvenile detention center. He'd made a name for himself at Eastern Michigan, too, where he ended up serving as special assistant to the provost. At the University of Michigan in Ann Arbor, he was the community liaison to the Office of Minority Affairs Advisory Committee. Perhaps most important of all, he developed a program to encourage gifted minority students to enter the teaching profession. As a part of this effort, Tom starred in an EMU video called "Slam Dunk for Teaching."

Why does he do all this? The most obvious answer is that he knows how beneficial knowledge is to a community. Speaking philosophically, Tom states that "information is without value until a community of learners receives it, reflects on it, and makes it a part of their lives. Then, and only then, does it become knowledge."

The Eastern Michigan community decided to show its appreciation for Tom, so with the help of a $50,000 W. K. Kellogg Foundation grant, they created the Thomas A. Fleming African American History and Literature Collection. This three thousand–volume collection is accompanied by a Web site and a lecture series whose theme is "Become a Person Who Reads."

Tom says, "As I read, I became a new person, a better person—more culturally aware, more intentionally seeking answers to the personal and social challenges of African-American life."

Over the course of his career, Tom has proven that he is up to these social challenges. It is his belief that education will help young men and women to overcome. If only more teachers shared that belief.

"Nobody else wants to touch these kids," says Dale Rice, a special education professor at EMU. "They've become so hardened over the years, there's just no way to get through. But Tom gets through. . . . He's a very honest person and you feel you can trust him completely."

Tom will tell his students, "I'm just trying to get you in touch with what you can do. . . . But this is a 50-50 proposition. I cannot teach you if you don't want to learn." His philosophy of classroom management goes hand-in-hand with this approach. He says, "Authority is conveyed not by assuming a controlling manner, but by active listening and by developing the ability to interpret student behavior."

Interpreting behavior means that brutal words spoken to a fellow student can be a cry for help and that being disengaged in class can be a test of trust. With most of his kids, Tom has answered that call and passed that test. One former student even achieved fame as an actor and a writer on TV's *Saturday Night Live*. A. Whitney Brown was on the show from 1985 to 1991 and dedicated his book, *The Big Picture*, to Tom. That's a far cry from deciding that school just isn't worth the time.

"I dropped out of school mentally around age thirteen, and physically at sixteen," Tom tells his students. When they are out of earshot, he says, "The greatest reward I find in teaching is the hope I feel when students begin to change."

Anyone who works with teenagers knows that the decision to change has to come from within. Even when done with some prompting, it is important for the student to feel as though he or she made the decision. The greater the buy-in, the better the chances of success. For understanding that education is indeed a 50-50 proposition, but that sometimes you have to give 110 percent to get that 50 percent, Tom deserves a university library named in his honor. He deserves recognition for having the most unique story of all the A+ educators.

In His Own Words

If I had to do it over again, I would still become a teacher. Teaching is hard work, but its personal rewards are priceless.

Of Ghosts and Double-Wides:
Maine's Brittany E. Ray

—————— *Educational Philosophy* ——————

"The way you get meaning into your life is to devote yourself to loving others, devote yourself to your community around you, and devote yourself to creating something that gives you a purpose and meaning."

—Morrie Schwartz, in *Tuesdays with Morrie*

Maine's 2007 teacher of the year works her magic in a double-wide trailer that a truck unloaded in the school's parking lot a few years back. Although at first this might seem funny, a second or two of thought should be enough to wipe the smile away.

Brittany E. Ray teaches English at Narraguagus High School in Harrington, Maine. She is a graduate of prestigious Colby College, yet she has to work in a trailer. In a parking lot. "It's hard to teach out there sometimes," she says. "There's no bathroom. There's no place to wash your hands." Narraguagus was built for 175 students but is now home to almost 300, thus the need for the double-wide. And that's no punch line.

Life gets no less interesting for Brittany at home. The last house she lived in was supposedly haunted by the ghost of her great-great-grandfather. This was one reason the people at *Extreme Makeover: Home Edition* decided to build Brittany and her family a new home. Other reasons are that her husband also works in the schools, that they adopted a daughter from China, and that their son has autism. Couple all of this with Brittany's life in the lot and you get the sense that there is never a dull moment.

"Outstanding teachers maintain enthusiasm even in the face of adversity," she states unabashedly. "Most importantly, teachers committed to excellence recognize the importance of reflection. Reflecting on students, classes, materials, successes, failures, and more ensures that we continue to grow."

To help her students grow, Brittany writes narrative progress reports for parents. These provide much more insight than mere grades, and it isn't all that surprising that an English teacher would use the written word to communicate. And clearly Brittany is a bright lady. She was the valedictorian at Colby College, a school with a tradition of producing "teachers and preachers." The idea to individualize reports to parents grew out of her experiences with special education, as a teacher and then as a parent. "When I first sat on the other side of the table as a parent, my whole world changed, and I knew from that moment on I would never participate in another PET [Pupil Evaluation Team] with those blinders on again. Because of the journey with my son, I am undoubtedly a better teacher and more compassionate to individuals with challenges. I make it a point to make parents feel comfortable advocating for all that their children need."

Growth isn't just for the students, according to Brittany. "Indeed, the exciting thing about a philosophy of education is that it is always changing and growing. . . . In my classroom, the most dominant element of my philosophy is to meet each student at his or her own level and move forward."

Even as Brittany and her colleagues try to move forward with their students, they worry about the important issues facing schools like Narraguagus. "Sadly, I think the increased emphasis on testing has taken on a life of its own that is far too often detrimental to schools and students," Brittany laments. "When snapshot-style testing can determine whether or not a student is eligible to graduate from high school, we are leaving students behind."

There is no quit in her, though. Like a scientist, she follows up on her problem statement by hinting at a hypothesis. "As teachers, we must guard against allowing tests and testing preparation to dictate the flow of learning in our classrooms. It is essential to keep in mind that the students need exposure to a wide array of educational experiences and not just those deemed valuable because they appear more frequently on standardized tests. I believe that we must be imaginative and find ways to improvise and leave the script when preparing students for tests. Moments when we can go off course, explore alternate strategies, and seek learning opportunities that personally connect with the lives of students will, in the end, promote greater student learning."

Brittany goes to great lengths to promote learning, especially higher learning. During the summer, she helps students by holding mock college interviews and by arranging transportation to college interviews. She gives the kids feedback on their college essays and helps them and their parents wade through all the financial aid paperwork. "They're frightened to apply to colleges with high tuitions. I really want to get the message out that my senior year at Colby I went for under $300 that my parents could contribute, and the rest was my own and scholarships. I want them to know that in the end, going to an Orono or to a Colby or a Bates might be the same financially."

Sarah Kennedy, a former student and valedictorian, says, "Ms. Ray has a unique ability to help every student realize his or her full potential. The faith and energy she invests in her students is reciprocated again and again as they graduate and move on to fulfill this potential."

Brittany also works hard to help fellow teachers, and future teachers, fulfill their potential. "Instead of shoving her lesson plans at me," says Ken Martin, a colleague and former student teacher, "she encouraged me to explore what I was interested in and to develop my own ideas."

One of the many things A+ educators have in common is helping people become all that they are capable of becoming. Whether they live in a trailer or are educated in one, it doesn't matter. What matters is the work of each individual and the individualized attention the teacher gives to his or her kids. For being a model of this kind of effort, Brittany Ray doesn't need any kind of extreme makeover, just maybe a classroom worthy of an A+ educator.

— *Advice for Teachers New and Experienced* —

I believe that teachers should avoid the "I am master" approach and work to facilitate growth by posing critical questions, tolerating ambiguity, exploring real-world situations, encouraging student decision-making in assignments and assessments, and always being open to alternative ways of thinking.

The ARC of Success:
Connecticut's Christopher Poulos

— *Advice for Teachers New and Experienced* —

As teachers we must reflect as to how students learn best, we must think about how we can improve our instructional strategies so that learning is meaningful and that all students are made to feel successful. For if we focus on our teaching and the learning needs of our students, no child will be left behind and those test scores will come regardless.

Some people criticize alternative certification programs designed to get people into the classroom as soon as possible and with as much support as possible. These critics will have a hard time making their argument after reading about Christopher Poulos.

Chris, Connecticut's 2007 teacher of the year, teaches high school Spanish in a nice little town called Redding. Before stepping into the role of suburban high school teacher, though, he spent more than two years in the Peace Corps, working in a small village in Honduras. His focus was community development and environmental education and one project he and his sixth-graders worked on was constructing a tree nursery to help reforest the community's watershed. The spark was lighted and after returning from Central America, he enrolled in Connecticut's Alternate Route to Certification Program (ARC). Chris was on his way to becoming a teacher.

Seven years after entering the classroom, Chris became the first graduate of the ARC program to win teacher of the year. Such programs train professionals from other fields for life in the classroom. Chris was a quick learner, and is even an adjunct professor of Spanish at Fairfield University now. He also served on the staff of the Rassias Foundation's Accelerated Language Programs at Dartmouth College and is enrolled in the University of Connecticut Administrator Preparation Program. But his classroom at Joel Barlow High School is really where it's at.

"He's the greatest Spanish teacher," cheers Leah, a former student. "He always has us do interactive stuff like oral presentations in front of the class or talking to other members of the class rather than just writing things down.'"

Another example of Chris's out-of-the-box thinking, when it comes to designing units and lessons, is the work he does with his upperclassmen. "I have developed a Spanish course for seniors in which each student designs and implements a volunteer project during his second semester. In lieu of traditional coursework and a final exam, students spend their time volunteering in Spanish-speaking organizations where they can experience language and culture firsthand. By combining learning with volunteering, students not only learn about the subject matter, but also begin to understand the importance of community service before they leave high school." Apparently you can take the man out of the Peace Corps, but you can't take the Peace Corps out of the man.

He admits it, too. "The idea is to re-create a mini Peace Corps experience. Redding is a New York City suburb, a well-to-do community where the children are not exposed to much diversity. By engaging in this type of community project, students not only learn Spanish, they also learn the value of service. Every teacher thinks his subject is the end-all, but ultimately I want to teach students to be good citizens involved in their community."

This kind of experiential education lets kids really buy into what they are learning. The sense of ownership and responsibility grows as they do things like translate for Hispanic patients at local hospitals and for a law firm that does pro bono work for battered Hispanic women. Some of the students even sing in a Hispanic church choir. The term "immersion" has one definition for the layperson and another for teachers of foreign languages. The layperson might envision the immersed student as one who is really excited about, and involved with, the subject. For Chris, immersion is a pedagogical approach that boils down to all Spanish, all the time.

"As a foreign-language teacher," he explains, "I believe in a total immersion model of instruction in which all lessons, activities, announcements, and daily routines are conducted solely in the target language. While it may be quicker and easier to explain a grammar point in English, learning becomes more meaningful for the students when they realize that they understand the explanation in Spanish."

One gets the sense that, despite his allegiance to immersion, Chris is not a control freak. For example, when asked what the most critical issue facing schools today is, he states that it is student involvement and empowerment. "Examples of student participation in school improvement include, but are not limited to, student input on mission-statement committees, conversations between the administration and seniors in high school regarding graduation requirements and reasonable special privileges during their final semester, and student council representation at steering committee and board of education meetings. This trend of increasing student input and participation is viewed by many as a means of improving school culture and making education more meaningful for students."

The students appreciate Chris's faith in their abilities and were happy to throw some love his way after learning of his teacher of the year award.

"It's cool that he won," says a former student named Dan. "He deserves it. He cares about his students. He knows who's on sports teams and he wishes us luck. He jokes around with us. . . . He's hard but he's a good teacher. I've learned more in one semester with him than in a whole year with some other teachers."

"He is most qualified to be honored with this award," says Superintendent Allen Fossbender. "He cares deeply about students. His mission is to empower them to believe in themselves and help them reach their potential. He celebrates their success and if they falter, he is there by their side."

Chris has a lot of faith in his students. This is evident in one of his favorite quotes, borrowed from the mission statement of the Comet Hill Primary School in Victoria, Australia: "Excellence can be achieved if we . . . care more than others think is wise. Risk more than others think is safe. Dream more than others think is practical. Expect more than others think is possible."

Chris expects a lot, empowering his students while pushing them to fully immerse themselves in the subject matter. It's a delicate balancing act, but one he has managed to pull off. This is why, despite following a non-traditional path to the classroom, Christopher Poulos ranks among the A+ educators.

--- *Compliments to the Teacher* ---

Megan, a former student and member of the student council, says, "He has touched many people's lives. He's a friend, a supporter, a mediator, a volunteer. Quite simply, he is the best there is." And, in a rare instance of accord, child and parent are on the same page. Her father, Lou, adds, "He's a great guy."

Monte and the Hi-Herald: North Dakota's Jennifer J. Montgomery

In Her Own Words

We all need to be a part of the solution-oriented promotion and improvement of public education, not only because it's good for business and the national interest, but because it's good for kids who need to find their way in the world.

Bismarck High School's Jennifer Montgomery calls it the way she sees it—a strategy that surely benefits her journalism students.

"I admit it," she says with a sigh. "I struggle to refrain from rolling my eyes at pithy teacher devotionals and classroom posters that exhort students to pursue boundless dreams and ever-ascending achievements. Those fortune-cookie phrases may look good on glossy posters of sunsets and sailing ships, but they lack the behavioral road maps that promote genuine student achievement. I prefer instead to teach students to embrace reality and their power to shape it, skills that enable the discarding of empty tasks in favor of focusing on worthwhile ones that lead to substantive achievement."

Jennifer is more interested in helping the students become self-motivated than in spurring them on with clichés and hollow sentiments. She projects the same air of disdain toward another group that speaks loudly and with little substance. "The rhetoric of many politicians and analyzers serves to advance careers and ideologies rather than to promote genuine and profound student learning." Authentic learning is possible when America's schools are supported and not just told to produce better and better test scores. Despite all this tough talk, Jennifer does speak fondly of the schools.

"I am proud to be a product of a great American public school. I am proud to be an educator in a great public school. . . . Children may not know it and may even deny it, but they are counting on us all to create for them schools and broader learning communities that build permanent and powerful foundations of knowledge, character, and humanity."

"To my great gain," she says, "my educational life has been filled with many more experiences with teachers and professors who love their work rather than the opposite. As important as the conveying of their subject matter, equally important to me was the attitude and the ardor they brought to the act of teaching and learning."

Biographically speaking, Jennifer has had some amazing experiences in addition to those amazing teachers. With two bachelor's degrees, a master's degree, and doctoral coursework at Harvard University, she is a model of educational pursuit for her students. Surely the kids have also noted that Jennifer, a National Board Certified Teacher, was a finalist for National Teacher of the Year in 2003 as well as North Dakota's teacher of the year. She has taught homeless adults and children in Grand Forks and used her background in Russian to teach Bosnian refugees. In her more than fifteen years of teaching, she has received a Milken National Educator Award and an Award for Excellence in Teaching from American Councils for International Education.

Jennifer put her teaching skills to use as a trainer in the National Education Association Women's Leadership Training Program. She also puts her journalism skills to use at Bismarck as her students produce a newspaper called the *Hi-Herald*. The monthly publication has a circulation of approximately 1,500, impressive for a school paper.

Continuing on the theme of public education and community involvement, Jennifer practically pleads, "Teachers and other educational leaders—be they parents, administrators, businesspeople, politicians—must move student-centered agendas forward in coalitions of common interest. Everyone in our communities who cares about children needs to care about the community-wide educations our children receive."

Doing her part to meet this obligation to kids, Jennifer pays particularly close attention to what they like to tell her about. "As a teacher, when students engage me in discussions of fishing or rap music or *Star Wars*, none of which interest me very much, I try to give them my full attention and my respect for their capacity to be passionate about their interests." Jennifer says this also serves as an invitation for her students to reciprocate and share her passion for English. To further promote friendly relations, she is fond of giving her students nicknames. Colleague Jane Pole says, "That's a great way to develop a rapport with kids. It's a great way to point out they're special enough that you picked out that trait in them." It was Jane who nominated "Monte"—you can't give nicknames without willingly accepting one of your own!

When a classroom-management issue comes up, Jennifer tries to handle it in a way that maintains student dignity. She aims to "deal with the problem, and then let it go." Oftentimes the message is sent without emphasizing the bad choice that was made. Jennifer gives her students credit enough to understand what they did wrong. This kind of environment, she feels, is the best way to ensure success. "Safe, supportive learning environments and authentic, interactive learning are essential to student success."

The nicknames are fun, and the classroom management instructive: sometimes the advice she gives falls right between the two. For example, she says that "every student should learn how to buy a good used car at a fair price. That covers a lot—research, analysis, interpersonal skills, decision-making, and self-control. It's one of those catch-all things that can be applied to any situation." Not only does this advice have an immediate benefit, but she hopes it also creates a good habit that will carry on into adult life. Given the nation's credit concerns, this kind of fiscal responsibility should probably be taught more often. Jennifer understands this because she has a journalist's instincts, not to mention a whole heap of empathy for her kids.

"Helping young people find their way in the world is one of the greatest contributions a teacher can make," she says. "Strong, enthusiastic, powerful teaching has more impact on student learning than any other factor. Because of that, top teaching will always be the biggest key to student achievement."

She has become a top teacher by combining a teaching tool of old with one that now permeates schools across the globe. "The Socratic method of questioning is a time-tested winner. Some great learning happens with a lot of open-ended questions. I also love the Internet with a good projector." Socrates and Google—each oracles of their own time.

Open-ended questions lead to discussion and debate, and Jennifer says, "What I would like for students is that they embrace conflict in a respectful way. I just think it's all about growing and thinking and rethinking throughout your entire life. It never stops."

Productive conflict might seem even more strange than the combination of the Socratic method and the Internet. But in capable hands, anything is possible—a saying that might look good on a poster, but not in Jennifer's room. This is one A+ educator who has no time for words unless they are going to lead to higher-order thinking or be included in next month's *Hi-Herald*.

Educational Philosophy

When Hillary Clinton chose the African tribal proverb "It takes a village to raise a child" as the core idea of her book about effectively nurturing children, some pundits spewed righteous indignation that she should dare extend the shaping of a child beyond the parents' own hands. I vividly recall being mystified at that backlash: of course it takes a village to raise a child, for better or for worse. I am proof of that, and my teaching is, as well.

Teacher, Speaker, Author:
Ohio's Sharon M. Draper

In Her Own Words

As a child, I taught my dolls, my dogs, and the kids next door. I never wavered in my desires and determination to become not just a teacher, but a really good teacher who made memories in the minds of children.

"If none of you choose to go into education, to make a positive difference in the lives of children who are not even born yet, who will be there to guide them, or direct their minds through the beauty and complexity of the vast wealth of knowledge that we now control?" Sharon Draper once asked a crowd of prospective teachers.

In conjunction with this message, Sharon wrote a book titled *Teaching from the Heart,* in which she prods prospective teachers toward the classroom by asking them about those teachers who stand out in their memory: "The kindergarten teacher who was not afraid to give a hug when needed? The history teacher who showed you the world of humanity? The science teacher who showed you how the physical and the natural world worked together to give us life on Earth? The music teacher who showed you that a complete individual needed a full complement of expression?" She then adds, "Somewhere in your educational career, one or more of these outstanding individuals opened your mind and showed you the way."

As a teacher, Sharon aims to be an outstanding individual for her students, whom she tells, "I teach because I need you as much as you need me. I teach because once upon a time a teacher made a difference in my life, so I am here to make a difference for you." And the difference she has made is enormous. In 1997 the Council of Chief State School Officers and Scholastic Inc. named Sharon the forty-sixth National Teacher of the Year. At the time, she was teaching English and language arts at Cincinnati's Walnut Hills High School, and she now has been working with young people for more than thirty years. Her husband is also a teacher.

"In Sharon's classroom, learning is real," said Dr. Ernest Fleishman, senior vice president of education at Scholastic Inc. "Her ability to help students comprehend the complex relationships that exist in the world merits her selection as National Teacher of the Year."

"I survived the Draper paper" is a motto that seniors in Sharon's class put on T-shirts after completing her required research paper. The pride in that statement is obvious and, apparently, deserved!

"Just as Plato instructed Aristotle, who taught countless others, as educators, the cycle of repeated learning and imparted wisdom is our burden and our joy to continue. I have learned as I taught, for I feel that an active learner is the best teacher," says Sharon, who without a doubt practices what she preaches. In addition to winning the national teacher of the year award, as well as Ohio's teacher of the year award, in 1995 Draper was among the first group of teachers to be certified by the National Board for Professional Teaching Standards. She was also elected to its board of directors. She has traveled to Russia, Ghana, Togo, Kenya, Ethiopia, Bermuda, and Guam, where she addressed large audiences about her craft.

Speaking to crowds comes easily to Sharon. She has her classroom experiences and is now a motivational speaker. She visits schools across the country to discuss teaching, but she has another reason to travel and talk. Sharon is a *New York Times* best-selling author. To date she has published more than twenty books and has been honored by the American Library Association with its Best Book for Young Adults designation. Sharon also is a five-time winner of the Coretta Scott King Literary Award, and her essay "The Touch of a Teacher" was published by the Center for Policy Research/National Governors Association in "What Governors Need to Know About

Education." The writing fits into her notion of living life as an active learner. Just as she gives, she gets.

Sharon tells audiences the secret of her success: "I see rainbows where others see only rain." In turn, "a good teacher smiles while she's teaching. She smiles because she is comfortable not only with her subject matter, but also with her classroom and her students." This kind of comfort earned her the National Council of Negro Women Excellence in Teaching Award, the Ohio Governor's Educational Leadership Award, and the respect of the people she so frequently addresses.

"You visited my school today," one student wrote in a letter. "I loved that assembly. You are so energetic and funny. I thought you would be old like the ladies at my church." It's easy to imagine Sharon's chuckle after reading that line. Then perhaps a humble tear as she read, "While I was reading your books, I was looking forward to silent reading, every day." This was from another fan, a girl Sharon had not met but whose life she had obviously touched.

For touching the lives of students, audiences, and young readers all around the world, Sharon Draper has earned widespread respect. It almost isn't enough to call her an A+ educator.

Educational Philosophy

"The major public education issues today are the same issues that are affecting and destroying the larger society," says Sharon. For her, these issues include apathy, poverty, and violence, and all have been touched upon in her writing.

Life, Liberty, and the Pursuit of Technology:
Missouri's Eric Langhorst

——————— *Educational Philosophy* ———————
I'm not trying to create a spark—I'm trying to start an out-of-control forest fire of learning.

This might be the age of text messaging, but there are still enough notes passed in class for one of Eric Langhorst's favorite tricks to work. "What's this?" he inquires after picking up a note from the classroom floor. Everybody wants to know.

That note is Missouri's 2008 teacher of the year taking yet another creative approach to teaching social studies to his eighth-graders. This lesson in particular has nothing to do with paying attention in class or using proper grammar when writing to a friend. That business is for the English teachers. What Eric is concerned with is teaching his students at South Valley Junior High School about the Declaration of Independence. He laments that his classes rarely understand the purpose of this historic document, so stumbling across this supposedly discarded paper is his introduction to the greatest "note" ever sent in U.S. history. After picking it up, he puts the words of the Declaration of Independence in terms they can understand, presenting it to the students as a breakup note. After all, didn't the colonies have to "break up" with King George before forming a nation? Because of Eric's creativity, after this lesson they all understand how things went down in 1776.

"Students enjoyed coming to his class because he could relate history to us," recalls a former student named Anna. "He knows so much about history and was just bursting at the seams with excitement about getting to teach it." To hear that quote makes it even easier to picture Eric in front of his class, note in hand, his voice rising as he reads the list of grievances. "He" did this! "He" did that! And then leading up to the grand finale as Eric announces that the colonies-turned-states "are Absolved from all Allegiance to the British Crown, and that all political connection between them and the State of Great Britain, is and ought to be totally dissolved!"

Not wanting to be limited to the archaic practice of passing notes, Eric is also in touch with cutting-edge technology. He publishes his lessons as podcasts—the Declaration of Independence lesson is podcast #120—and has more than 150 of them available online. He serves on the district's technology team and works to expose his students to the academic possibilities of blogs and podcasts. One year Eric had his class read the book *Guerrilla Season* and then used blogs to communicate with the author, Pat Hughes. A class in California studying the era in which the book is set got in on the action, too, making the experience all the more meaningful for Eric and his kids. So groundbreaking and successful was this unit, and the manner in which the two classes and Hughes used technology to work together, that the story was featured in *USA Today* in November 2006 and then in the *School Library Journal*. Two years later, Eric was recognized as the top teacher in the state. After winning the award, he wrote, "One thing I'm very excited about is the opportunity to discuss the potential of the Web 2.0 classroom with a broader audience, and I can't wait to spread the potential of blogs, podcasts, wikis, etc. to a variety of people."

Brad Armstrong, principal at South Valley, says, "He's an innovator in the use of technology and helping kids understand the concepts of American history and make connections at deeper levels."

Beth Felice, of the Missouri Humanities Council, adds, "Eric Langhorst uses the rich media and communications tools of the Internet to amplify his teaching and engage students in his classes, as well as students and teachers around the world."

Eric wasn't always on top of his game. Once upon a time, he subscribed to the idea that knowledge is a pitcher of water and a student's brain, a vase: open up and pour all that information right in. He admits, "I thought the best teachers were the ones who could cram as much knowledge into students' heads as possible. Quickly, I discovered that the secret is to engage students so they leave your classroom asking even more questions."

Attention-getters like picking a note up off the floor can entertain students only for so long. There has to be substance to the lesson if it is to resonate. Eric is smart enough to know this, is motivated enough to want to prepare his kids for what the modern world will require, and has gone to great lengths to make the tools of technology part of his curriculum. Clearly he has found the right balance. One moment he is talking blogs, the next he is running off for a meeting of the Clay County Historical Society Board of Directors. One minute he is connecting his kids with students in California, the next he is coaching the eighth-grade boys' basketball team. With one foot planted in the past and the other in the future, Eric exemplifies what it means to be an A+ educator. The times call for these kinds of teachers, and these truths we hold to be self-evident.

In His Own Words

When asked what he hopes to accomplish on a daily basis, Eric replies, "Teaching about George, Thomas, and Abe using the latest technology."

Tough Love:
Washington's Tamara Steen

Every teacher sees homework as both a means and an end, but for Mabton Junior-Senior High School's Tamara Steen, that end is slightly different than it is for most. Homework is less about student efficacy and more about an individual piece of data that tells a bigger story.

"I assume full accountability for whatever happens in my class-room. If students do not complete their homework, for example, I analyze the cause(s) of the problem, focusing on how I failed to scaf-fold them to success. I then report my conclusions to my students and ask for their feedback. I take their suggestions into consideration and then present my solution to the problem."

This kind of attention to detail won Tamara Washington's teacher of the year award in 2005. That she is an excellent teacher who helps students reach tremendous heights earned her a spot as a finalist for National Teacher of the Year. At the time of her national recognition, Tamara had been teaching for twenty-three years. She teaches English to students in grades nine through twelve and even her Advanced Placement class doesn't have the makeup of the typical AP class. "The irony is that the students I serve in my Advanced Placement Eng-lish classes are chronically underserved in advanced courses across the United States. I work in a school with a 95 percent Hispanic popula-tion and with an 85 to 90 percent poverty rate. . . . During the entire

2007–08 school year—without 'dumbing down' the curriculum—only 5 percent of the grades were Fs." That statistic says a lot about Tamara's students, but also about the way she chooses to teach. For example, if she had a less stringent policy about homework, the failure rate would probably be much higher. Everything makes a difference in the end.

A philosophy is at work here, and Tamara's pedagogy is one part melting pot, two parts American dream. She says, "I also never presume to judge what any child is capable of, which is the reason so many migrants have the courage to take my advanced English classes. They know I will walk every step of the way with them, even if it means tutoring before or after school."

It was in one of her non-AP twelfth-grade classes, however, that Tamara interacted with a student whose story would become Tamara's definitive moment as an educator. She writes, "In January of 1999, I discovered a senior in my basic English class could not read. I knew her reading level was listed at the fourth grade, but she lacked the phonics to read beyond the most basic, familiar words. She had by that time completely given up and was failing English. I told her we could fix her problem. She came in during the lunch hour for the next two weeks and I taught her phonics. At some point during each session, she cried, and when I finally asked her why, she replied, 'I feel so stupid.' I didn't say anything, but the next day I read the children's book *Thank You, Mr. Falkner* by Patricia Polacco, a story of an elementary student who could not read and felt stupid. Then her fifth-grade teacher realized she had dyslexia and taught her how to read through a different method than anyone had tried with her before. The little girl grew up to be the author of the book. When I finished I asked my student why I had read that story to her. She looked me straight in the eye and replied, 'Because you want me to know I'm not stupid.' She never cried again. Six weeks of lessons later, she was reading a part from Shakespeare's *Hamlet* and explaining what she had just read to the rest of the class. Her grade in my class skyrocketed to a B, and she still keeps in touch." You can tell that this contact makes Tamara happy, but the next detail is what makes her proud: "Today she loves to read and is reading to her children."

One of the other special things Tamara does is distribute an evaluation to each student at the end of the year. Yes, the students have the opportunity to give the teacher a grade. One student summed it up best when he wrote, "You give too much work, your work is too hard, and nobody wants to do it. But somehow you manage to inspire us to do it."

Continuing on with the idea of accountability, Tamara turns the focus back on herself. "I never release control of my class to the students by blaming them for being 'lazy and unmotivated' or that they 'need to be held accountable'—nor do I allow them to use excuses, either. The work we do is too important."

Lest she be perceived as uncaring, it's wise to consider that perhaps the tough teacher cares more than the laissez-faire teacher. In relation to this notion, Tamara says, "Love, when combined with discipline and high expectations, is a powerful thing."

Tamara has tremendous faith in what her kids are capable of—it's just that sometimes things get in the way and the student needs to be nudged back in the right direction. The worst thing a teacher could do, she believes, is coddle students and allow them to get away with petty excuses. Imparting this lesson to new teachers, Tamara says, "Never underestimate any student's potential because it is not our right to determine a child's future. The eighth-grade math student who flunks algebra may grow up to be another Albert Einstein, and the sophomore athlete who is eliminated from the basketball team may grow up to be another Michael Jordan. The student who cannot shut up may be a future president of the United States, the student who thinks the homework is too boring to complete may invent the cure for cancer, and the child who cannot sit still due to ADHD may win the Nobel Prize for literature. How do we know what they are capable of becoming as adults when they are only six or thirteen or seventeen?"

Tamara is serious about this, too. She adds, "It is our duty to look at our students through the eyes of love, seeing not who they are today, but what they may become. We must believe in them so strongly that our belief becomes contagious—and they catch it. All of them."

"Love, when combined with discipline and high expectations, is a powerful thing," Tamara says. "In a school like mine—and likely any school—high standards and creativity will not by themselves produce the results I want. Students need to feel connected; some are so wounded by life they cannot begin to function academically until they realize a teacher actually cares about them personally. Sometimes we as teachers must even be willing to be surrogate parents." It is because of this extreme dedication that Tamara Steen is an A+ educator.

In Her Own Words

Educating children is an avocation for me, as well as a vocation. I am passionate about the art and craft of teaching, about teaching teenagers, and about teaching English.

Coach, Teacher, Advocate, Friend: Kansas's Joshua M. Anderson

——————— *In His Own Words* ———————

Passersby in the hallway usually hear us learning well before they see us learning!

In 2007 there was little debate over who was the best teacher in Kansas. That honor went to a teacher of speech and debate and of language arts, hailing from Olathe Northwest High School: Joshua M. Anderson.

Josh works with students in all four grades, and in his ten-plus years of teaching, he has also taught forensics. However, debate would seem to be the area where his heart and soul reside. He is skilled in debate, and the highest praise comes from a former student and debate team member.

"The debate room has, over the past three years, become much more than just a classroom. It's a gathering place, a discussion forum, a makeshift locker, and above all else, a refuge," says Jesi. "If I tried to put into words exactly what Mr. Anderson has done for all of us, it would sound trite and clichéd. He's our coach, but he's also our teacher, our advocate, our strongest supporter, and our friend. . . . In twenty or thirty years, I probably won't remember how to calculate the cosine of an angle or what protein phosphorylation is, but I *will* remember what it means to live with great character and integrity— not simply because of the rigorous expectations he has for us, but because I have seen it modeled firsthand by Mr. Anderson himself."

Josh is one of the few A+ educators to have a somewhat troubled past. As a kid he wasn't teaching dolls or asking for a chalkboard for Christmas. "They say that teachers can never find a good name for their own kids because every suggestion evokes the name of some devil child. That was me," he says with a laugh. "I was that child. For most kids, sixth grade is a time of discovery and imagination. For me, sixth grade was about the time my teaching career really started to take off. Using all the best practices an eleven-year-old prepubescent punk could muster, I pitted the boys against the girls (small-group learning), stood around the hateful children on the playground (proximity control), and frequently failed to turn in my work (modified assignments). Yes, it was the start of a promising career as a classroom teacher."

These days Josh coaches a debate team that has been ranked No. 1 in the nation and is working toward a master's degree in school leadership. He is upgrading his school's technological capabilities so effectively that he won the "Top 100 Wired Schools" Facilitator Award from the *Princeton Review* and *Family PC Magazine,* which recognizes outstanding and innovative use of classroom technology to improve student achievement. Not bad for a "prepubescent punk"!

Given his own experiences as a rabble-rouser in the classroom, Josh has put great thought into his strategy of classroom management. The approach can be called courteous. "Every visitor is welcomed with a round of applause, and it is not uncommon for students to spontaneously applaud each other for good questions and answers. Students who accidentally interrupt another student who is speaking are expected to walk over to that student, shake hands, and ask for forgiveness."

Accountability is important for Josh. It begins with, but is not limited to, his students. "At strategic intervals throughout the year, we will stop as a group and assess our progress. Students are asked to read each indicator carefully and rate themselves on a scale of one to five using reflective questions based on the staff development model adopted by the state. A subsequent classroom discussion helps us establish conclusions about where we have been and where we need to go. Copies of the curriculum indicators we have mastered are also sent to the parents periodically for their review."

This is in line with Josh's philosophy of education. He explains, "What is needed, then, is a model of accountability that gives teachers the room they need to develop a personalized pedagogy . . . while simultaneously requiring clear evidence of academic growth for every child."

"What makes Josh a master teacher," says his principal, Dr. Gwen Poss, "is his ability to develop in students the responsibility for their own learning."

Josh expands on this compliment with: "It is impossible, however, to demand the best from my students unless I provide a support network that ensures that any student who is struggling is identified early and surrounded by other members of the village who are prepared to offer meaningful support because they already know what it's like to live in the village."

It is this concept of "village" that motivates Josh to open himself up to the community in which he teaches. He wants taxpayers to know what they are getting for their money. He is proud of what his students are achieving and thinks that good news ought to be shared. "The most important part of our job as teachers is to introduce the community to our students and our students to the community. To do this, we must live in both worlds." To this end, Josh sends out a weekly two-page e-mail newsletter that includes a summary of the previous week's work and details what will be done over the coming week. "The newsletter even includes specific 'dinner table questions,'" Josh explains, "that parents can ask their children at home to check for understanding."

Josh also has faith that informing parents as to their child's progress, or lack thereof, is also worth the time. "Another technique that I use to keep the village together is progress reports e-mailed to parents every week. If assignments are missing, parents can consult the newsletter to learn more about the assignment requirements. Counselors, coaches, support staff, and administrators also receive e-mailed progress reports for their students and use them to keep track of each child's academic standing." This well-thought-out system has reaped obvious rewards for Josh's kids.

It is a team effort of which he says, "The most effective and active classrooms in schools today are those that encourage collaboration among parents, teachers, support staff members, administrators, and of course the students themselves."

Promoting collaboration and caring has left a lasting impression on former students. A young man named Cory says, "Mr. Anderson— I have so much to thank you for, it's hard to know where to begin. As a teacher, you inspired me. I found that I am capable of doing so much more than I thought I could. As a friend, you spoke up at a difficult time. Your few words helped me see myself clearly. You are a great teacher and a great friend, and I will never forget you."

This is the kind of relationship Josh works hard to build. He admits, "While the curriculum determines our daily activities, it is our culture and climate that determines our success. Good teachers know that students who clearly understand expectations and who feel emotionally and physically safe are more empowered to take an active role in their learning."

Josh doesn't just talk about involving families and the community, he does it. He doesn't just talk about having the students play an active role, he facilitates it. These are the things A+ educators do for their kids, and Josh does them exceptionally well.

In His Own Words

We are in danger of becoming a national institution purely devoted to producing empty children with outstanding test scores.

A Musical Director with Natural Command: Utah's Kim Schaefer

——————— Compliments to the Teacher ———————

How is she going to come into this high school class comprised mostly of burly boys, all noodling away as loud as possible on their respective instruments, and take control? Schaeffer, 32, marches her tiny body through the chaos and up to the podium. She starts conducting a brisk 4/4 rhythm. She holds up one finger, then two, then three: the notes of a concert B-flat scale. One by one, the students notice Schaefer, stop jamming and start playing the indicated note. Within about a minute, she has the entire band's attention without having uttered a word.

—www.navajotimes.com

Once upon a time, Kim Schaefer graduated from high school in a ten-person senior class. Today she lives in a traditional "hogan" on a Navajo reservation in Montezuma Creek, Utah, where she teaches music to grades seven through twelve at Whitehorse High School. In 2007 the small-town music teacher made big news as she was named Utah's teacher of the year.

"Learning the musical language was challenging," Kim says. "I learned how to learn, how to deal with obstacles, how to express myself, and how to persevere. Being in a school music group gave me a place to belong; the band members depended on me to be there and to contribute all that I could. These feelings are what I want to share with young people."

Kim was the first high school music teacher in Utah to achieve National Board Certification. Though all too often the arts fall by the wayside in districts with limited funds, Kim has fought to keep her program alive, and under her leadership it has not only survived, it has flourished. Montezuma Creek is one of the poorest areas in the United States, as almost 100 percent of its students receive free lunch and 95 percent of the band's students use musical instruments the school provides. It might be a small school, with approximately 300 students in grades seven through 12, but when one considers that almost half of the school is enrolled in a music class, that's a lot of instruments. Recalling her plea for more public support, Kim tells a story about stopping in the middle of a school concert to hold up a broken saxophone. She said to the audience, "Look at the kind of instrument these kids are playing! They deserve better." Her tactic worked.

Kim has been at Whitehorse for eleven years. She is your typical go-getter, serving as a School Leadership Team Member, a new-teacher mentor, and secretary for the School Community Council. She is the chair of the Utah Music Educators Tri-M Music Honor Society and has served as a panelist for the Utah Arts Council Panel. Most impressive of all is that Kim has volunteered nearly five hundred hours teaching free music lessons to her kids. In addition, she established an instrument scholarship program, in which students can receive their own musical instrument through a competitive process.

"She comes in weekends when we need extra help," says Arwin, a student who plays oboe. "She knows where we all live."

Kim explains, "I accept students at current skill levels and help them to learn more than they thought possible. . . . I also design learning experiences to allow for student-paced learning." She adds with a smile, "My ultimate goal is to train Whitehorse High School's next music director."

That said, Kim has no plans to get off the reservation any time soon. She is a teacher who loves her job. "The best thing a person can do in life is finding something they enjoy and doing that. I have found that in teaching—it's hard work but it's fun, every day."

Recalling all of her accomplishments over the past decade-plus, Kim shows her competitive nature in one particular memory. "My students used all of their potentials and earned a Superior-minus rating at the

2006 State Concert Band Festival, the highest rating ever earned by our school at State!" It was quite an achievement for everyone involved.

"I think of learning as a spiral," Kim explains when asked about her philosophy of education. "The learner is constantly reviewing previously acquired information while approaching new information. I believe the deepest learning occurs when students have a reason to apply knowledge and skills to real-life situations."

Spiral learning and applied learning are two ways of addressing an important concept for Kim: student engagement. She says, "There is an increasing number of children who act out in school, disconnect from learning, or who fail to make academic progress." What could the solution be? Kim thinks that "public recognition through performances and presentations is one path to student engagement, plus these are considered 'real-life' and authentic learning. As a result of real-life learning, young people will be better thinkers and problem solvers because they are calling upon deep structure knowledge and integrating new academic concepts while serving in their community."

Although she teaches music, Kim knows the importance of attaching academics to her units of study. All six of her band classes, for example, use a listening journal "in which they listen to a recording and then write down a description of the music, including tempo, tone, and mood. . . . As part of No Child Left Behind, every teacher is supposed to incorporate writing into their curriculum. I tried to think how I could do that without giving up any music teaching time." The strategy worked and she has seen both the students' writing and music appreciation skills improve.

A special teacher is able to touch her students' lives while reaching out to the community. Kim has achieved this dual goal. As participation in her music program has grown, so has the respect and support of colleagues, parents, and those charged with minding the purse strings. A teacher who can achieve that, in addition to getting every student to play nicely and in perfect harmony, deserves to be called an A+ educator.

"How Are You Doing?":
Minnesota's Mary Beth Blegen

Mary Beth Blegen is one quotable educator. Mostly this is because
she understands the profession—and people. One of her gems that is
fairly well-known amongst excellent educators is: "Instead of alcohol
and drug counselors and educators asking, 'What are you doing?' we
need to ask, 'How are you doing?'" That could almost be a philosophy
unto itself. How are you doing?

Mary Beth's point is that in this age of high-stakes testing and
technology-induced overexposure—what is the purpose of Facebook
and MySpace if not to find out "What are you doing?"—adults need
to check up on *how* their kids are doing as much as the kids are checking up on one another. Her quote also seems to be a political statement, of sorts. She is begging authority figures to worry more about
the cause than the symptoms, to put more resources into curing society's ills than punishing them.

This kind of reflective thought, focusing more on the big picture
than minutiae, earned Mary Beth the honor of Minnesota Teacher of
the Year and subsequently National Teacher of the Year. As a representative of her profession, Mary Beth has an impressive biography. Over

the course of three years, she served as the first teacher in residence with the U.S. Department of Education. As part of her responsibilities, she ran the National Teacher Forum, an annual meeting of more than one hundred of the nation's top teachers to discuss issues affecting American's schools. She was the keynote speaker at a meeting of the Coalition of Essential Schools and has been published in *Education Week*. Returning home, Mary Beth was named blueprint coordinator for Saint Paul Public Schools in an effort to create small, nontraditional, student-centered learning communities in seven urban high schools. A good question for Mary Beth is "How are you doing *it*?" The answer: with love, energy, and over thirty years of experience.

A question like, "What are you doing?" can yield some pretty interesting answers, especially when the respondent is a person like Mary Beth. She has worked with teachers in Japan, Ukraine, and Lithuania as well as twice working with American teachers studying Mozart in Vienna on a grant from the National Endowment for the Humanities. Who wouldn't want to have a conversation with someone like that?

So impressive is Mary Beth's résumé, it takes awhile to get to what she actually teaches. At the time of her national honor, she was a history, humanities, and writing teacher at Worthington Senior High School in Worthington, Michigan. Returning to the more important "how" questions, Mary Beth admits, "My philosophy of teaching has changed. Oh, we still read and discuss and write and argue. But we talk more about the 'why' and 'how' of learning. The students ask more questions and I try to give fewer answers." This fits in with her goal of finding common ground with kids; of addressing them in their world. Mary Beth advises educators "to meet kids where they are, not where we think they should be." She truly wants to walk a mile in her students' shoes. She understands that this is the way teachers have to approach relationship-building in today's world.

"It's when kids and I work together that something happens—that ideas take shape," she says. "My goal is to expose kids to a multitude of ideas and situations while asking them to connect, create, and analyze."

In a letter to a former student who is now a teacher, Mary Beth wrote, "The kids you see every day need you to be their advocate. They need you to be fearless in your desire to make sure that our schools are places created for kids and places where their being known and their learning come first." For all teachers, she says, "We need you to push the profession to do things differently. We need to reach beyond your classroom to challenge the profession and the teachers in it to get better."

For working so hard to help teachers and students to better themselves, for bothering to differentiate between such questions as "what" and "how," Mary Beth Blegen has been recognized as one heck of an A+ educator.

Educational Philosophy

We are here to help students develop skills that will carry them into another century, which promises to be no less revolutionary than the Industrial Revolution of the late eighteenth and early nineteenth centuries.

Achieving Great Heights: Montana's Steve Gardiner

——————— *Educational Philosophy* ———————

Steve's teaching has been influenced by the concept of flow, developed by psychologist Mihaly Csikszentmihalyi. Flow is the "state in which people are so involved in an activity that nothing else seems to matter."

In Latinized Spanish, *Montana* means mountainous, and it's hard to imagine Steve Gardiner living somewhere other than Montana. Mountain climbing is one of Steve's passions. Fortunately for the students at Billings Senior High School, another of his passions—one of many—is teaching.

Although you get the sense that Steve could teach any subject he set his mind to, he has been teaching English and journalism to kids in grades ten through twelve for thirty years. Not only was Steve named Montana's teacher of the year for 2008, in 2002 he earned his certification from the National Board for Professional Teaching Standards. For most people, recognition like this would be like finally reaching the summit, but for Steve that summit is more literal. To say he has achieved great heights isn't just a figure of speech.

Steve is quite an athlete. He has run the New York City Marathon, as well as the Boston Marathon, and is the coach of Billings's cross country team. What gets people's attention, though, especially that of the students, is when he talks about the mountains he has climbed. There is Mount Kilimanjaro, Mount Aconcagua in the Andes, and finally Mount Everest. Not merely a teacher, mountain climber, and marathoner, he has published more than five hundred articles in such publications as the *New York Times*. He has also published a book on teaching and three on mountain climbing. Steve's book *Under the*

Midnight Sun told of an expedition to Greenland in which he and his teammates located the world's northernmost land and in doing so, became the first humans to cross four glaciers. Somehow he also finds the time to advise the yearbook club.

Steve also makes time for charity. He is involved with 50 for Tibet, a group that is raising money for Tibet by climbing the highest mountain in each of the fifty states. He also has helped raise funds for a hospital in Kenya. In reflecting on how his interest in international travel and community service has benefited him, Steve says, "Because I have traveled the world, I have an expanded sense of community."

Traveling the world to climb mountains, run marathons, and help others sets quite an example for his students, and he likes to model good habits for them, such as engagement and passion, reading and writing. "I demonstrate most skills for my students, including reading with them, discussing reading as an active reader, sharing my own writing (published and unpublished), and even by running all the workouts I assign to my cross country team. . . . Modeling is the way every child learns, from how to tie a shoe to how to drive a car."

Although he reads out loud with his kids, he also knows the value of quiet time. He uses sustained silent reading (SSR), in which his students spend the first fifteen minutes of each class reading a book of their own choosing. He even wrote a book for the Association for Supervision of Curriculum and Development called *Building Student Literacy Through Sustained Silent Reading*. One of Steve's favorite teachable moments came during SSR and, in this case, it was the teacher who learned from the student. "In my first year of teaching, I was beginning a program of sustained silent reading. One day I was giving instructions to a group and a boy asked me to be quiet because I was taking up their reading time. . . . I have hundreds of success stories which came out of that comment made in my classroom in 1977."

The kids are comfortable with Steve, but not audacious. "His students have a respect for him that is almost reverent," says colleague

Judy Barnes. "They win awards; they publish; and most of all they grow as I have never seen students grow."

Success begets success, and those involved soon come to see the world through an optimistic lens. This is true of the teacher and the students. In this particular case, Steve feels about his job as most good teachers do: that it is built on a foundation of hope. He says, "We work in cycles—six weeks, semesters, years—and we get to start over regularly. We get to try new things and perfect old things and watch students grow. It is a profession based on optimism, on knowing that life and work can always be improved and made better, and we work with students who are continually looking toward the future. What could be more happy, more inspiring than that?"

Given the great heights he has reached, it almost isn't enough to call Steve an A+ educator. For his students, he is more than a teacher. He is achievement personified.

In His Own Words

Over the years, I have published five hundred articles and four books, and these have become important parts of my teaching style. My students see these publications and know I can help them with their writing and reading. My runners know I've run the Boston Marathon and New York City Marathon, so I can help them learn more about running.

A Child of History:
Oklahoma's Mitsuye Conover

Mitsuye Conover is an incredibly strong person in that she is able to take painful aspects of her life and turn them into valuable lessons for her students. Every history teacher hopes past mistakes will never again be repeated.

Mitsuye was born in a Californian internment camp during World War II. She spent the first three years of her life there, remained in the United States after the war, and went on to attend California State University. She earned her master's degree from Northeastern State University and has spent more than thirty years teaching high school social studies. Her efforts earned her membership into the National Teachers Hall of Fame and the Mid-America Education Hall of Fame. When the time comes to teach the unit on World War II, it is easy to picture the faces of her students as they learn this interesting detail from their teacher's life.

It is harder, though, to gauge their reactions when Mitsuye shares the other painful event. Every year on the anniversary of the death of her son, Sean, Mitsuye discusses it with her classes. A drunken driving accident caused her son's death, and she hopes that the personal approach finally gets the message across to those who think themselves immortal. Ever the teacher, Mitsuye even asked the judge to order the man who killed Sean to go to his grave with her on his birthday every year for seven years. The judge agreed. Hopefully, the lesson is learned. "I always tell my students about Sean. If you can get through to one person, you're a success. You don't want your child to have died in vain. I feel obligated to try. . . . I tell them this happens to real people. We're not talking about someone else. We're talking about your teacher."

And what a teacher she is. In 2000, Mitsuye was named Oklahoma's teacher of the year and a few months later was named a National Teacher of the Year finalist. Everyone involved with Bartlesville High School, where she had been teaching for the past five years, was proud, though not necessarily surprised.

Margaret S. Butler, the parent of a former student, says, "It was through Mitsuye's influence that my son began thinking about moral, social, and political issues. She helped him develop the critical-thinking skills necessary to be a good citizen in our society."

Continuing the theme of connecting the professional and the personal, Rita Baird, executive director of elementary instruction for Bartlesville Public Schools, adds, "Mitsuye Conover transforms a normal classroom into a stimulating interactive environment in which students connect the concepts of history to their personal lives and prior knowledge base. Mitsuye involves her students in stimulating dialogue, role-play, debate, dramatization, research, and writing. The students internalize the concepts that have been taught, and it genuinely becomes their own learning." And from a former student named Amanda: "Like a waterfall of wisdom pouring into a river of respect, Mrs. Conover is a teacher with a deep, undying devotion to her students and her studies."

Then there is the history itself. "My main hobby," she says, "is collecting antiques. It goes with my teaching so well. It kind of justifies it. They are my teaching tools. . . . I don't think I thought that when I started, but now my hobby has become my resource." It's easier to reach great professional heights when you are not only interested in your work but also believe that work is important. Given Mitsuye's own personal history, how could it be any other way?

"Our country is very great, but only when it works correctly. Hopefully, we can learn from the past. . . . I really believe in what I'm doing," says Mitsuye. "I can tell people what happens when we lose our rights."

Mitsuye knows that doom and gloom grabs attention but that there has to be more pizzazz if she is going to keep that attention. That's why, in addition to having her class put on historical plays, she has been known to dress up as historical characters. Rather than turn her back on life, Mitsuye has chosen to embrace it and to share its lessons with kids. Give her an A+ for that!

Educational Philosophy

For three decades, Mitsuye has worked in the classroom, teaching children about their history. She has also tried to impart her passion to future teachers, as well, giving talks to teacher prep programs. Just as she challenges her kids, she challenges her audience. For example, one talk she gives is titled, "How Much Do You Want to be a Teacher?"

How Do You Say "Heterogeneous" in Arabic?: Vermont's Michele Forman

Educational Philosophy

Without mutual trust, students are wary of accepting the risk and vulnerability of learning. For them, the threat of feeling or appearing inept or incompetent is best overcome with the support of a teacher in a caring, accepting, and respectful relationship.

Middlebury, Vermont, is a college town, and a high school social studies teacher there tries to bring collegiate learning into her classroom. Although Middlebury High School is just a typical small school nestled into the mountains, that teacher was able to bring not just statewide but nationwide attention to the school in 2001, when Michele Forman was named Vermont Teacher of the Year and then National Teacher of the Year.

"Through time spent working with her in the Arabic Club, in the Student Coalition for Human Rights and above all in class, I have developed enormous respect for and admiration of Mrs. Forman and all of her work," says Timothy, a former student. "She is respected by all students who have taken a class with her. Nearly all have felt inspired by her teaching."

Michele designs lessons that are intended to inspire kids to look further and learn more. One project is a simulated hearing on the New York City Triangle Shirtwaist Factory fire of 1911. In teams of two, thee, or four, students take on the roles of the factory owner, floor manager, workers, fire department, and so on. "They research the fire using a broad selection of primary and secondary sources," Michele explains, "only some of which I provide. As a class we interview the teams one at a time. Each team attempts to determine blame for the deaths of the workers and defend its own role in the tragedy. Each

129

team is evaluated on its defense, both through its research materials and notes, and on the team's use of evidence and reasoning during the hearing. In addition, each individual student is evaluated on an analytical essay that addresses the same question: who was to blame?"

The students get excited about the various aspects, and as with any group project, they must tap into their strengths to contribute. When the groups interact as a whole, history comes alive and, more often than that, Michele can watch the lesson's goal come to fruition. "I want my students to understand that historians use many lenses to construct interpretations and analyses of our past."

At the White House for the National Teacher of the Year ceremony, Gordon Ambach, the executive director of the Council of Chief State School Officers, said, "Michele has the exceptional combination of a sharp and creative intellect, a commitment to help students address the major political and human rights issues of our times, and the personal warmth that nourishes growth and confidence in her students."

In a subsequent interview, Michele said, "Teaching is a creative endeavor and I believe it's OK to color outside the lines. For example, one of the reasons I chose to learn Arabic was that increasing my students' understanding of the Arab culture through that language could powerfully decrease the stereotypes many of them held of Arabs and Muslims."

With her interest in Arabic and the world at large, Michele now advises the Arabic Club, which meets before school, and she is involved with the Student Coalition on Human Rights. It's one thing to design an innovative project, but it's quite another to go out and learn a foreign language. Living in a college town makes sense for a lifelong learner like Michele. She continues to push herself to new heights, but that is the life she has always led. At one time she was a Peace Corps volunteer, working in Nepal. Back at home, she worked as an alcohol and drug education curriculum specialist for the Vermont Department of Education and served on its Task Force on High

School Reform. She had earned respect on the state level as a teacher of high school health. She also became the first teacher from Vermont to earn National Board Certification in adolescence and young adulthood for social studies and history.

There are many skills in Michele's bag of tricks, but for teachers just entering the field or looking to recharge their batteries, she says, "A good teacher needs not only a good understanding of what he or she teaches, but also a sense of excitement in learning and a clear vision of how the key elements of a subject can be conveyed to students." It is good to remember that "each student is a unique person and a powerful learner capable of great achievements. I truly marvel at my students' capacity for learning, accomplishment, and growth."

In the never-ending effort to tap into that most abundant of natural resources in any school—the students—Michele advocates heterogeneous grouping. By putting together classes that consist of kids achieving at all different levels, possibly dealing with different barriers, such as a disability or English as a second language, lessons in difference can be taught hand-in-hand with the curriculum. "Education is enriched for all students," Michele says, "when learners bring their different experiences, perspectives, and skills to the group." Citing her success, she adds, "For ten years I have advocated for and taught classes with students grouped heterogeneously by perceived ability. Learning is enriched for all students when learners bring their different experiences, perspectives, and skills to the class. . . . I find that the depth and thoughtfulness of discussions increases over those in homogeneously grouped classes."

Richard Seubert reveals more about his talented colleague: "Along with high expectations, she cares for them as human beings first, which helps kids appreciate their potential and set goals that push them to higher levels. She doesn't talk down to them but promotes a dialogue which honors their ideas and celebrates their uniqueness as human beings." To hear all this talk of dialogue and discussion makes it fairly easy to picture what a vibrant classroom Michele must lead and to envision the level of engagement she accomplishes with her students.

"Teaching is complex and dynamic, demanding constant reflection and adjustment," Michele says. "My students and I work collaboratively toward the common goal of learning."

For being such a strong proponent of differentiated instruction and difference within the classroom, Michele is teaching the lesson all social studies instructors hope to impart over the course of the school year: that the greater world is a much more diverse place than your hometown. Given how Michele has been able to get Middlebury's students ready for that greater world, she is not just an A+ educator in the Green Mountain State but on the national level as well.

— *Advice for Teachers New and Experienced* —

"Our profession is one of the few that eats its young. We often fail to properly prepare and support new teachers. Good teachers are uniquely individual and we must nurture and support each new teacher as that person develops," Michele says. When asked to list possible solutions, she mentions "strong mentor programs, peer observation programs, team teaching, and co-planning."

Transition Camp and a Second Chance:
Virginia's Thomas R. Smigiel Jr.

———————— *A Defining Moment* ————————

Late last school year, the superintendent came to one of my leadership classes and asked my students what they wanted to do after they
graduated from high school. It brought tears to my eyes when two
students raised their hands and said that they wanted to motivate
students and be a leadership teacher just like Mr. Smigiel. That is my
greatest contribution to education.

Nobody works harder than Thomas Smigiel Jr. to keep kids in school.
Thomas uses the same passion and vigor to go after the freshmen at
Norview High School in Norfolk, Virginia, as he does to attack political issues. For him it's all about community. By trying to affect the
political process, he can improve schools and even the neighborhood
where he lives. His home state of Virginia showed its appreciation
when, in 2008, he was named teacher of the year.

At Norview Thomas is the coordinator of Freshman Transition
Camp, a form of orientation aimed at giving new students a warm welcome and the kind of practical information that eases the switch from
eighth grade to ninth. Thomas is driven to make the camp a success
because, he says, "from my experience and research, the underlying
cause of increasing high school dropout rates is the lack of motivation on the part of ninth-graders to succeed and make lasting connections." He was motivated by a Boston College study that said the rate
of ninth-grade dropouts had tripled in the past thirty years. A *Time*
magazine report highlighted that one million American students drop
out of school every year. "This is a national problem," Thomas says.
"We have to do something about this crisis now." Research shows that
the most effective solution is providing smaller learning communities

and making sure each student has a connection with at least one adult in the building.

There is also a need to address failure, as this can often lead to a lack of self-esteem and interest. Thomas started a program called Second Chance, which offered night school for freshmen who had failed a class. In the first year, all fifteen students in world history passed their Standards of Learning Test, while 80 percent of the students taking English and mathematics passed and were able to move on to the tenth grade. They moved up and did not drop out.

Thomas teaches teen leadership and earth science to ninth- and tenth-graders, and as part of his leadership curriculum, he gets his students involved in community service and fund-raising. "In the last two years, my students have helped raise over $10,000 for Operation Smile, SPCA of Norfolk, Amyotrophic Lateral Sclerosis Association (ALS), American Cancer Society (ACS), Food Bank of Southeastern Virginia, and the Hope House Foundation."

The story of how Thomas first became interested in teaching is different from any of the other A+ educators. His desire was born of physical violence, inflicted upon him by eight boys when he was a sophomore in high school. One boy in particular piqued his interest. Thomas explains, "When I went to court to testify against him, the judge asked him why he did it; the boy responded that it was because I was white and they had nothing else better to do. It turned out that he also had a very long criminal record and he was only sixteen. After that incident, I changed as a person. I wanted to know how a kid just one year older than me had such an awful life and did such awful things. It was from that point on that I knew I needed to be a person who influenced change." Thomas was obviously a very mature sophomore, able to see beyond the violence and get to the heart of the matter. This act had less to do with skin color than where that boy had been and where he was heading.

It is this kind of maturity and perspective that enabled Thomas to be nominated for a Disney Teacher of the Year award in 2002 and six years later to be named a National Teacher of the Year finalist. At that point, Thomas was eight years into his journey down the education path. At Norview he has served as yearbook adviser, is active in mentoring and writing curriculum, and helps his school to host the American Cancer Society's Relay for Life. Outside of school, Thomas has put time into cleaning up the neighborhood around his home, so the city council appointed him to the Norfolk Environmental Commission. He is also politically active with the Virginia Education Association. It is the students, though, who receive the lion's share of his effort.

Thomas says, "We must advocate for our students by being a voice for them and communicating their stories of empowerment, resiliency, and success."

One story that should be communicated is the work he did with a troubled young man named Mark. "Mark is a student who does not have a positive relationship with his father. Mark was getting in a lot of trouble, doing drugs, and failing his classes until he met me. Mark's English teacher recently handed me a paper entitled 'My Role Model,' in which Mark had written about how I had impacted and changed his life. When I think I am just doing what I normally do, I get surprised with a wonderful write-up from a student about how I helped him."

And how does all this helping come about? Thomas puts in the time to get the students what they need. On top of that, he impacts the learning of other students by working with their teachers. He explains, "I helped create lesson plans that met the needs of all students and worked on strategies to help close the achievement gap. I helped bring the pass rates on Virginia's Standards of Learning (SOL) tests up from 49 percent to 84 percent. From my experience, I was able to mentor earth science teachers across the school district and teach strategies so that they could have success in their classrooms.

"Teachers who fail to improve, whether from poor preparation, burnout, or lack of professionalism and who are judged to be ineffective must be counseled out of the profession in order to ensure students' success in school," he says. But Thomas prefers to focus on the positive. "This consequence should only be the last resort of accountability after the steps listed above have been taken. Accountability should be viewed as positive support as well. We need to offer recognition and incentives for good teachers. We need to focus more time on positive attributes of effective teachers and not get bogged down with always addressing the ineffective teachers. Keeping accountability positive will help retain quality teachers and help teachers strive for success. Positive feedback will keep teachers motivated and encourage more teachers to share their success with teachers who might need it and benefit from their success."

It is important to keep freshmen in school for the next three years, and it helps when there is a low staff turnover rate and when average teachers get better and better.

"Truly remarkable outcomes are possible in a classroom when trust, respect, and caring relationships are allowed to flourish. Think about how communicating a message of building positive relationships could change our education system! I believe we can repair our dropout issue by not only continuing our rigor, but also by capturing our kids' hearts and giving our students personal attention. Let's focus less on a 'one size fits all' approach to teaching and more on 'one student at a time' teaching."

Given that he actively reaches out to freshmen, and that he relishes the opportunity to help colleagues as well, Thomas gets the kind of grade he hopes his students will earn—an A+.

Educational Philosophy

One of his favorite quotes is from Flip Flippen of the Capturing Kids' Hearts program: "If you have a child's heart, you have his head."

Teaching Is Aerobic:
North Carolina's Melissa Bartlett

Although it might sound odd, Melissa Bartlett earned her credentials as an English as a second language teacher in Cairo, Egypt, as a result of the master's degree she received from American University there. In 2003, Melissa was named North Carolina's teacher of the year; so talented is she in teaching ESL and language arts that she was even named a finalist for National Teacher of the Year in 2004. Six years before, she also achieved National Board Certification.

At the time of her teacher of the year award, Melissa was teaching students in all four grades at Statesville High School. She has taught for more than twenty years, and her résumé is impressive. She began as a Peace Corps volunteer, teaching math, science, physical education, and conflict resolution to children in northern Africa. She also taught remedial reading to students in the U.S. Virgin Islands. In total, she taught for eight years abroad. This kind of experience, coupled with the awards, earned her a spot as an adviser to the state Board of Education. She was also a member of Governor Mike Easley's Teacher Advisory Committee.

Teaching is clearly a passion, and as if her day job wasn't enough, Melissa has also taught community college classes and aerobics at the local YMCA. She invites her colleagues to come take her class, which makes sense given that surviving the school year is no easy task. Certain elements of teaching definitely require stamina, and the school year itself is more marathon than sprint.

Of her teaching philosophy, she says, "Learning is a natural behavior. It's just a matter of doing what you can to bring it out." The "you" in that statement is quickly replaced by a more communal pronoun. "We must take ownership of and nurture our educational institutions. By 'we' I mean parents, teachers, students, presidents, legislators, CEOs, business owners, retirees—everyone should have a vested interest in what goes on in our schools; after all, it is where our future spends most of its time five days a week. I would encourage volunteerism and activism as means of supporting education. I also encourage people not to be satisfied with what they hear or read, but to go into schools to see all the good things happening there and how they can help. I would also urge people to support the educational needs of their communities even in the face of economic downturns because without education, a society's prosperity is even more difficult to achieve and maintain."

So proud is Melissa of the work she and her fellow teachers do, she had no problem taking then education secretary Rod Paige to task over comments he made about teachers in general and the National Education Association in particular. Paige referred to the NEA as "the coalition of the whining" and a "terrorist organization" and in a meeting with all the state teachers of the year he found himself seated next to Melissa, who took the opportunity to slide a button in front of Paige that said, "I am the NEA!"

No mere antagonist, Melissa is willing to put in the work to make schools better. This includes standing behind a Working Conditions Survey aimed at improving professional development. The creation of the survey was a shared decision-making effort between teachers and lawmakers in North Carolina. Their goal was simple: figure out how to do a better job of training one another in how best to serve our kids.

Lest she be painted as too focused on schoolwork, it is interesting to note that Melissa never assigns homework on the weekends. She also knows not to give homework when there is a big schoolwide event. Melissa is a highly motivated educator, but she's also in touch with her students' lives.

"She was always relaxed. She always let us try and figure out things before making her own suggestions," says Stephanie, former editor of the school literary magazine, for which Bartlett serves as adviser. Humility is a key ingredient in great teaching and although she is very talented, Melissa displays very little ego (despite pushing that button at Rod Paige!).

"It was first thing in the morning," a former student named Martha recalls about Melissa's class, "but nobody fell asleep. It wasn't like a normal class. We got up and moved around. Nobody was watching the clock, waiting for it to end."

In Melissa's classes, there aren't just students from all different grades, there are students of all different abilities, ethnic backgrounds, and economic situations. This does not negatively impact her teaching. As colleague Deborah Ellis puts it, "She has a perspective on cultural diversity that few have. She speaks two or three languages fluently, and her classroom decor is travel—the students love it." Her classroom might be in North Carolina, but Melissa knows the value of showing her kids the world she has been fortunate enough to experience. Language, culture, and history are like foods to be tasted and she serves as the chef. Even more than that now-famous moment with the NEA button, this is why Melissa is an A+ educator.

In Her Own Words

I think that if I could wipe out all of the inappropriate professional development I've sat through and only attend that which I and my school really need, I wouldn't be so concerned about the use of time for it. Outcomes-based, data-driven professional development would create the balance we need.

Civilization Begins Anew:
Virginia's Philip Bigler

─────────── *In His Own Words* ───────────
The American public schools have become the modern-day battle-ground with the classroom teacher engaged in a vital struggle to bring intellectual enlightenment and cultural enrichment to his students.

When asked who influenced his decision to teach, Philip Bigler quickly names two people. He recalls that in the eighth grade, Sister Mary Josephine taught him a love of learning, and in high school it was Colonel Ralph Sullivan, an ex-Marine, who showed him there is always more to know and another book to read. "To follow in their footsteps," Philip says, "and to help young people in the same ways that my teachers had helped me is both a privilege and an honor."

In 1998 Philip honored the efforts of Sister Mary Josephine and Colonel Sullivan when he was named National Teacher of the Year. A teacher of humanities and history at Thomas Jefferson High School for Science and Technology in Alexandria, Virginia, Philip was the forty-seventh educator to earn this award and at the time had been teaching for more than twenty years. He almost didn't make it to the classroom, but after spending two years as the historian at Arlington National Cemetery, he remembered those early influences and got his teaching career under way. Philip also wrote four books, including *Hostile Fire: The Life and Death of Lt. Sharon Ann Lane* and *In Honored Glory, Arlington National Cemetery*. Philip won the Outstanding Teacher/Historian Award from the U.S. Capitol Historical Society and, better yet, he gets to go to work every day with his wife, who teaches Spanish at Jefferson.

Philip says, "In reality, our schools are just empty, impersonal places. It is the students, the teachers, and the principals who bring them to life and give them an identity. For a brief moment in time, these special people create a living, vibrant community of learners dedicated to the universal search for truth and, in Thomas Jefferson's words, 'the illimitable freedom of the human mind.'"

Philip likes to use quotes to convey thoughts from the past and, in turn, explain present situations. "An old proverb asserts that 'civilization begins anew with each child.' As an educator, I have found this statement to be both a vision of optimism as well as a dire warning. On one hand, our students are the intellectual heirs to Plato, Aristotle, Augustine, and Newton; the inheritors of a rich legacy of human progress traversing three millennia. Conversely, if we fail to successfully teach and educate our young people, we are just one generation removed from barbarism."

As an excellent teacher of history, he works to make past events and people come to life. In one unit, Philip has his students interview residents of the Soldiers' and Airmen's Home, asking elderly and disabled veterans about their World War II experiences. He hopes that face-to-face contact will generate lasting memories like he has of Colonel Sullivan and will bring to life the photos in a textbook the next time a student, fresh off a visit to the home, opens that book. Other attempts to bring history to life include making his students members of a Greek *polis* to debate the issues of the day, re-creating the Islamic pilgrimage (the *hajji*) to Mecca, and arguing the intricacies of constitutional law before a mock Supreme Court.

Although Philip feels like everything is well under control in his classroom, he does feel that there is reason for concern about the teaching profession. He says, "A school system's greatest asset is its teaching staff. Indeed, it is the classroom teacher who brings a curriculum to life, provides meaning to a subject matter, and inspires young people. As a result, the recruiting and retaining of quality educators has to become a major priority for all school jurisdictions." Once the recruiting initiative has been deemed a success, it is time to keep those teachers in school. "It is imperative that all veteran teachers provide a strong support and mentorship system for their younger, more vulnerable colleagues and take a proactive interest in their well-being." Not only is this good for the kids, it is good for the school. As a class moves up to the next grade, the receiving teacher pays a price if the students are not adequately prepared. Teachers count on one another for this preparation, as each teacher builds a foundation for the following year's learning.

"My greatest satisfaction as a teacher has been helping young people learn to love history and instilling in them a personal desire to seek knowledge," Philip explains. "My students soon appreciate that civilization rests upon the foundations of the past and realize they are inheritors of a rich, intellectual legacy."

For fostering this kind of appreciation in America's youth, Philip proves that he made the right decision walking away from Arlington Cemetery and into the classroom. Rather than tending to the past, he is working with the future. An A+ effort, for sure.

— Advice for Teachers New and Experienced —

In a letter to a former student interested in teaching, Philip wrote, "Take pride in being a teacher. I now know that teachers perform small miracles every day and have dedicated their lives to making a better future. As our principal at McLean used to say, 'To be a teacher is to be forever an optimist.'"

The Decisive Element:
Arizona's Kristin Bourguet

———————— *In Her Own Words* ————————

A teacher's mind-sets, skills, and actions are the most influential tool in sculpting the mind-sets, skills, and actions of students.

Kristin Bourguet is so much more than a ninth-grade science teacher. She is the cream of the crop.

When Kristin earned the distinction of being named Arizona's 2007 teacher of the year, the twenty-ninth teacher to be so named, ready to congratulate her was the twenty-eighth teacher, Beth Cirzan. Beth is one of Kristin's biggest fans and not just because they are both excellent teachers. Kristin and Beth worked at the same high school at the time of their honors: Marana High School in Tucson, the school from which Kristin graduated.

Of this returning alum, Beth writes, "Many teachers prefer to teach upperclassmen as both the failure rate and the challenges that come with teaching freshmen are much greater. That is not the case with Kristin. She is a teacher that really believes that all students can learn and be successful. . . . I might add that every student passed her class last year and she is indeed one of the most rigorous teachers I've encountered. Every day she goes above and beyond what is expected of teachers. I am one of many veteran teachers that regularly seeks out Kristin for support and advice."

Veteran teachers are wise to swallow their pride and ask for help from newer teachers when they possess skills like Kristin's. And Kristin believes teachers of great skill and experience must be funneled toward struggling schools. "Students who are behind need qualified teachers to move them forward. In order for our most at-risk students to have the teachers they need to catch up, a human resource reallocation needs to take place. By providing incentives for master teachers to teach in our schools with the greatest needs, there is hope that our at-risk students will have the single most important resource they need in order to close the achievement gap: quality teachers."

Kristin found success with her students when she first began to teach in Louisiana and then again in Arizona by always being there for them: before school, during lunch, after school. She made herself available to them for makeup work, tutoring, and quiz and test retakes. She also developed a program called GOAL, which stands for Great Opportunity to Achieve Learning. Her effort to close the achievement gap isn't a haphazard effort based on heart and soul and elbow grease. Kristin takes a methodical approach that begins with assessment. She says that early in the year, "I spend a significant amount of time administering diagnostic exams in an effort to meet each child at their intersection of challenge and ability." But it isn't all about tests and scores. "I take time to learn about the needs and interests of my students. In addition, I also solicit information about my students from their parents or guardians." Her ego isn't such that she immediately discounts parents. Just as veteran teachers know to invite her to the table, she knows to invite others to the table to help her students learn.

As a part of GOAL, she says, "weekly progress reports are issued in order to show students the effect that hard work has on their grades. These reports are shared with parents or guardians in order to keep them abreast of their student's academic performance. Partnering with students' families has been the cornerstone of the success I have experienced in the classroom." Kristin also employs differentiated instruction, cooperative learning, and problem-based learning. She adds, "Strategic grouping of students has enabled me to work with each student at their individualized instruction level. I work relentlessly to make sure that the topics we discuss are relevant to the students."

Her kids notice, too. A former student named Rhett describes her teaching as "crazy, but really cool." He adds, "She always makes it like real life. She puts crazy twists into it."

The feelings are mutual. "I am humbled daily by the power of our profession," says Kristin. "My work with my students has made me a better thinker, a daily dreamer, and a passionate believer that a good education can change a child's disposition."

When asked to relate her greatest accomplishment in the classroom, Kristin remembers back to her second year of teaching, when she was still working in Louisiana as the Environmental Architectural Design magnet program coordinator. "My students learned about advanced technological applications and used their skills to design and implement service learning projects throughout our community. We worked together to design, fund, and build a large greenhouse on our school campus. My students' efforts resulted in an invitation to the National Environmental and Spatial Technology Conference, where my students were awarded with the first-place award for project design. The experiences I had with my students in Louisiana inspired me to become a lifetime educator." It's hard to believe a second-year teacher could be so accomplished, but it's easier to believe that the one thing she thinks all children should know is the scientific method. Kristin believes in the five steps, from "name problem or question" to "report results," and says that once the scientific method has been mastered, "students can use it to work through future problems and challenges." That's what lifelong learning is all about and that's why Kristin is an A+ educator.

Educational Philosophy

One of Kristin's favorite teaching quotes, and one that has certainly influenced her philosophy of education, comes from a young teacher in Israel. "I have come to a frightening conclusion. I am the decisive element in the classroom. It is my personal approach that creates the climate. It is my daily mood that makes the weather."

Of Appalachia:
West Virginia's Rae Ellen McKee

———————— *In Her Own Words* ————————

My new title as National Teacher of the Year makes me prouder than ever to proclaim myself a teacher. I wear the armor of a professional. I am not embarrassed to vocalize the positive qualities of my profession, nor am I slow to defend it. It is not myself that I seek to champion, but the good that teachers do.

Rae Ellen McKee, the 1991 National Teacher of the Year, is a fifth-generation teacher, and her school, Slanesville Elementary School, is just ten miles from where she was born. Rather than leave this part of West Virginia, where she lives in Levels and works in Slanesville, and rather than break the mold of her family's vocation, Rae Ellen decided against attending law school and instead earned a master's degree in education from West Virginia University. Rae Ellen, who teaches remedial reading, is certainly one with the community in which she teaches. Her roots run so deep that her ancestors first set foot in the region more than three hundred years ago. This might be why President George H. W. Bush came to Slanesville Elementary to deliver Rae Ellen's award rather than having her travel to Washington, D.C.

Before learning that the president was coming to town, everyone assumed that Rae Ellen would be going to the nation's capital. "Are you really going to Washington to meet the president?" one student asked. When she said yes, the student seemed confused and said, "He doesn't need you. He can already read!" Before presenting Rae Ellen her award, President Bush told this tale, much to the delight of the crowd. And what a crowd it was. Rae Ellen's people turned out in droves to celebrate her.

"I am of Appalachia," she says. "That is why I chose to teach in West Virginia. I know her children. Two decades ago, I grew up with them. The children of the poor migrant and tenant farmers of the region were my neighbors, classmates, and friends. Now I feel I can help create a bright future for them."

Rae Ellen's father was a teacher and an administrator for more than forty years, so it isn't surprising to hear her cite his influence when discussing her career. "Through his example, I learned to be more than a teacher—I learned to be an educator. In my father's classroom, all children were equal because all had the ability to learn, perhaps not at the same pace or in the same language, but all could partake. Through his dedication, he showed me how much could be done to help all people, regardless of their situations, if interest and energy were directed toward alleviating barriers that kept them from reaching their full potential. . . . He taught me that any job that demanded much time was not worth doing unless you were bettering the existence of another human being. He insisted that his students, of which I was one, never stop growing or learning."

Gary Kidwell, principal of Slanesville Elementary School, recalls, "Upon her arrival at our school, she began to motivate our most disillusioned students to participate, learn, and enjoy her classes. Before long this excitement to learn became a part of these students' entire day."

The compliments are nice, but Rae Ellen has no time for hyperbole. She prefers to whittle the description of her work down to one simple statement. "I teach little children to read." It sounds easy, but anyone who has ever tried to do this, especially with an exceptional learner, knows that is far from the truth. Expanding slightly on the importance of her job, Rae Ellen says, "I hold the values of our culture and the history of our world before them like a sweet confection. I make them reach out and grab their education from me. I possess the power to lace their intake with arsenic or sweet nectar, creating their self-esteem or destroying it. I shudder under the burden of such a responsibility."

For giving this responsibility its proper due, Rae Ellen has earned the respect of her students and colleagues. For opting out of law school and deciding to carry on the family tradition of giving back to the people of West Virginia, there neighbors have decided to give her the title of A+ educator.

Educational Philosophy

I believe that the future of our nation depends upon our citizens' ability to think, rather than repeat learned information. Thus, education must motivate students to love the learning process.

Engineering Student Success:
California's Lewis Chappelear

─────── *A Defining Moment* ───────

At one point, when I noticed the cultural and societal gap between our teachers and our students, I decided to plan a teacher bus tour of our local community. Several veteran teachers commented that it was the most effective professional development they'd ever experienced.

This is the story of a man who went from earning degrees in biomedical and mechanical engineering to teaching in the Los Angeles juvenile system to gaining membership into elite aerospace and aeronautics organizations to earning national recognition in his field.

Lewis Chappelear's field is education, but the specifics of what he teaches make for something other than the usual teacher-makes-good tale. Lewis teaches engineering and design to students at James Monroe High School in North Hills, California. However, he started somewhere else entirely.

"My first assignment was in Central Juvenile Hall in downtown Los Angeles, one of the most secure and prisonlike facilities in the country," he says. "After going through several checkpoints, I got to my classroom. Each of my students wore an orange jumpsuit, and I felt like I was in a movie—a really scary movie. I asked where the books were, but there were none. I asked for some paper and pencils only to find out that the students were not allowed any object that they could use to stab each other or the teacher. What was I going to do? I spent the day just talking with the kids; it was one of the best days of my life. I loved it! They were real, living, breathing human beings who had been through more than I could ever imagine."

Like all educators, Lewis would have other moments of clarity, the kind of revelations that take their teaching to the next level. It was on a Sunday evening, while returning on a school bus to the school parking lot from a field trip, that he got another lesson in how deeply his passion for his students, and his profession, really ran. "There was what appeared to be a homeless woman being questioned for loitering by two huge police officers, one with his hand on a gun and the other holding a baton. Her clunker car was filled from floor to ceiling with unfolded clothing, broken boxes, and reused plastic grocery bags. There was only enough room in the backseat for a five-year-old girl and the cutest little one-year-old in a baby seat, both sound asleep. All the faces on the bus were fixed on this terrifying scene and a voice from the back of the bus yelled, 'Miguel, isn't that your mom?' This was that defining moment in my life when I knew I could make a difference in the world. Miguel was not only a third-year student in my class, but also our robotics team captain. He was intelligent, well-liked, responsible, and trustworthy. He exhibited leadership qualities rarely found in sixteen-year-olds. I thought I knew him. It all made sense now—why he wanted to stay late after school, why he went to the library until it closed every night, why he was always eating the food that I kept in my secret hiding place. Miguel was homeless. To tell you the truth, I was absolutely terrified at this newfound responsibility, but took it on and conquered my fears. I went into class, looked into my students' eyes, and started to see stories that have never been told."

Lewis took "this newfound responsibility" and ran with it. While learning about his students, they learned about him: his passion for robotics, his love of engineering, his interest in aeronautics and aerospace. And in 2007, Lewis was named California's teacher of the year. Then he became a finalist for 2008 National Teacher of the Year.

Despite the accolades, there is plenty of work left to do, and recently Lewis commented on the problems facing America's schools today. "In my opinion, the three biggest issues in public education today are the lack of rigor, lack of relevance, and lack of relationships. While most teachers would confidently say that these three concepts are of the utmost importance, many classrooms are missing them entirely. Every day is a symphony of rigor, relevance, and relationships inside and outside my classroom." This "symphony" is more commonly known as the new three Rs.

In describing teaching, Lewis moves from the symphony to Broadway shows. "The only way I can explain the profession to the nonteachers in my life is by using the analogy that it is like putting on a different Broadway show every day—a seven-and-one-half-hour show at that. This is not just a show to watch, but one of interactions with the audience members, who challenge, inspire, and encourage. It is a careful blend of improvisation and scripting, constantly morphing itself to fit the moment and never failing to surprise."

Although he loves his subject matter, Lewis cares even more about the art of teaching. He has soared to great heights, which is one of the reasons he deserves to be called an A+ educator.

In His Own Words

Teaching is about being an ambassador for humanity.

More than Just a Lab Geek:
New Hampshire's Carolyn Kelley

Compliments to the Teacher

"In the beginning," says a student named Kaila, "I honestly thought that I wasn't going to like this class, but about a week into it, I'm like, 'Wow, this is really cool!' I'm all science-y now."

Long gone are the days when science was a field reserved for men. As a science teacher at Seacoast School of Technology, Carolyn Kelley taught the boys a thing or two. That is one of the reasons why New Hampshire named her its teacher of the year in 2007. The list of reasons is long and says a lot about kids and education.

At the time of her award, Carolyn had been teaching biotechnology for nine years, working with sophomores, juniors, and seniors. She happily calls herself "a lab geek," but a true lab geek wouldn't really know how to teach other people. Carolyn has built her pedagogy around the new three Rs: rigor, relevance, and relationship. "Rigor means making sure that all students are being given challenging work, and then pushing them to do it," Carolyn explains. "Relevance means that their schoolwork relates to their goals and lives. . . . Lastly, by generating relationships with educators and with professionals in our respective fields we make the connection for our students that what they're doing now makes a difference to them and to others. Working with a teacher is often a student's first professional relationship, and a successful one gives them the courage to form additional ones."

Another reason why Carolyn is a great teacher is her skillful use of metaphors and analogies to help kids relate new material to their background knowledge. For example, when introducing a lesson on why not all bacteria produce acid after eating glucose, she pointed out that not everyone likes Mexican food, because not everybody likes spicy food.

At the time of her award, Seacoast's principal, Nancy Pierce, said, "The kids just adore her, and she doesn't make it easy on them. She doesn't have to give lots of quizzes to check on their knowledge, because she makes it so urgent that they know they need to learn this in order to do what they want to do."

For Carolyn, it wasn't just about what the students *had* to do in her class. It was about what they *wanted* to do down the road. "If you can show students how science is so relevant to their lives, they really grasp onto it. I'm graduating students every year that go on to science careers." Back in her Seacoast days, there was a Wall of Fame outside of Carolyn's classroom that focused on the internships she'd helped arrange for former students in such areas as studying genetics and working with the medical examiner's office on suicide trends. The wall also included information on what those students went on to study in college.

Vaughn Cooper, an assistant professor of microbiology and genetics at the University of New Hampshire, says of a former Seacoast student that in high school "he was a good student but not one of those blinding all-star students . . . but it's clear that the experience he got in [Carolyn's] classes . . . really lit a fire under him. When he showed up in my lab he started to swim right away."

"The unique thing about what she's doing," says Matthew, a former student majoring in microbiology, "is that she starts teaching a lot of high-level procedures that you probably wouldn't learn till you're a junior in college."

Carolyn also played an important role in expanding the number of biotechnology programs in New Hampshire: from one when she arrived in 1997 to ten programs less than ten years later. She is also "proud that colleges and laboratories have heard of my program and recognize the students who graduate from it as being of sound quality and of exceeding professional skills." In this era of accountability, teachers like Carolyn have nothing to hide. "Integrity, persistence, and a sense of personal responsibility need to be modeled by us, by school staff, by parents," she says.

Nowadays, Carolyn is modeling her brand of professionalism for a different crowd. She is back in the lab, so to speak, serving as the director of the Bristol-Myers Squibb Center for Science Teaching & Learning. She's still a teacher, though, working as a professor of microbiology at Connecticut's Quinnipiac University.

"The advances in biotechnology will help shape the world in the coming years," Carolyn states proudly, "and my students will be among the shapers. It is my mission to make a difference in my students' lives, but my students must also make a positive difference. Knowledge, service to school and community, and real-world understanding produce not only good scientists, but also good citizens."

For keeping kids interested in science and for working hard to produce good citizens, Carolyn has been recognized as a leading teacher in the field of science. Her mission is a noble one, helping to get kids "all science-y," as Kaila so aptly put it. Given the way she has already accomplished this mission, Carolyn is no mere lab geek. She is an A+ educator.

Educational Philosophy

Plan for it, work for it, and earn it.

A Mountaineer Forever Striving to Reach the Top: West Virginia's Eric Kincaid

———— *Compliments to the Teacher* ————

"Eric is a science teacher who is innovative and dynamic and infuses his students with enthusiasm—even building a life-size whale once as a teaching tool!"

—Joe Manchin, governor of West Virginia

Morgantown, West Virginia is home to West Virginia University, and over the past decade there has been a familiar face around campus. That face belongs to Eric Kincaid. Eric has learned a lot during his time as a Mountaineer, and every day, in some way, shape, or form, what he has learned benefits his biology students at Morgantown High School. That is one reason why he was named the state's teacher of the year in 2008.

"Teacher of the Year candidates must be able to inspire students of all backgrounds and abilities to learn," says Mike Lutz of Toyota Motor Manufacturing, one of the companies to sponsor the award. "Students respond when teachers show enthusiasm for their subject and genuine interest in the lives and success of their students. Eric Kincaid is an outstanding teacher who exemplifies the high expectations of the Teacher of the Year program."

Speaking of Morgantown, Eric earned both his bachelor's and master's degrees from WVU. He is also an adjunct professor at WVU's College of Human Resources and Education. In 2003 he finished the long process of attaining National Board Certification and is one of fifty educators to earn a national Siemens Award for Advanced Placement. From the fine people at Harvard University, Eric received the

Singer Prize for Teaching Excellence. He was actually nominated by a former student named Amy who was enrolled in Harvard's M.D./Ph.D. program. That's one way to say thank you to your teacher!

Eric operates the school's Health Science Technology Academy program, which offers participants the opportunity to receive full tuition to any West Virginia college or university. He also initiated the school's Advanced Placement biology program. Although the bulk of Eric's teaching is with juniors and seniors, he created a semester-long scientific continuum project for ninth-grade honors students. He knows that in a few short years, they will be juniors and seniors, so he does himself and his fellow teachers a big favor by getting them prepared now.

Eric's principal, Janice Goodwin, says, "Mr. Kincaid's enthusiasm for teaching is evident every day. . . . From murder mysteries and public health epidemics to building a life-size whale, Eric has demonstrated his ability to integrate science with other subjects, to develop student abilities, and to teach all children."

Eric is an innovative teacher who knows better than to try to force curriculum down students' throats. He meets them on their territory and tries to appeal to all different types of learners. "I have always believed that in order to really understand a concept, a person should hear it, see it, and do it, and that is what I try to do with the concepts I teach," he says.

Eric has been described as an advocate of learning by discovery, a goal any good science teacher shoots for with his or her students. Eric is a Milken Family Foundation award winner, and his biography on that Web site states that "Mr. Kincaid involves students in hands-on labs, distance learning, technology, team activities, and research." No wonder the governor—and everyone else—took notice.

Eric takes great pride in his work and often writes op-ed pieces. He felt compelled to address an editorial in the *Daily Mail* titled "W.Va. Should Concentrate: Students Need Fewer Initiatives and a Great Deal More Focus." Eric wrote, "What West Virginia has done is update its content standards and objectives to add rigor, relevance and 21st century skills to make sure our children graduate prepared for today's global economy, whether their plans include college or the workplace. We are doing this by aligning our standards not only with the National Assessment for Educational Progress but also with international standards found in the Program for International Student Assessment." He knows there is work to be done, but it obviously bothers him that people are all too critical of educators' efforts in West Virginia, especially in regards to school reform and educational achievement. Somebody has to defend those who are working hard.

If only more teachers would speak up, legislation on the state and national level might be more realistic, goals might be better designed, and morale might be as high as it should be for the group charged with educating today's children. Eric sees what needs to be done and is achieving it daily with victories large and small. For all he has achieved and all he is fighting to achieve in the near future, Eric deserves to be recognized as an A+ educator.

Compliments to the Teacher

"It is my distinct privilege to honor such a fine educator in our state's public school system. Mr. Kincaid's enthusiasm for teaching is evident every day. Innovative and dynamic in the classroom, he infuses students with tremendous motivation and instills in them a love for learning."

—Steve Paine, West Virginia superintendent of schools

Brown Is the Color of All Colors:
New Mexico's Tamra A. Tiong

In 2007 Tammy Tiong was a finalist for National Teacher of the Year. The news that Tammy, a special education teacher at Dulce Elementary School, was a finalist capped off a year in which she had been named New Mexico's teacher of the year. Not bad for a professional who had come into the field via an alternative certification program.

Tammy attended Northern New Mexico Community College for her Special Education Alternative License, and just eight years after completing that work, she was being complimented by the bigwigs in the state capital and then the nation's capital. Tammy broke into the field working through AmeriCorps as part of an environmental program and by teaching on the Jicarilla Apache Indian Reservation. Tammy says that teaching has always been in her blood. "I believe that some things are innate; otherwise it would be difficult to explain why, at three years old, I would sneak work sheets and books out of my big sister's backpack and hand them out to our stuffed animals—a virtual rainbow of dirty but well-loved creatures that had no choice but to attend my 'school' on the lower level of our bunk bed. I would even grade their papers with red crayon, drawing happy faces and stars when they tried their best. I secretly tried to learn from my sister's work and couldn't wait until I, too, could go to kindergarten." And now she teaches kindergarten.

To be more precise, Tammy handles special education for kindergarten and first and second grade at Dulce. A few years after Tammy stole her sister's schoolwork, a teacher stepped in to add fuel to Tammy's fire. "Mrs. Thoren managed to create a safe and embracing environment in which *everyone* enjoyed the journey of learning, whether they were traditionally 'low-performing,' 'gifted,' or simply 'too cool for school.' She had a beautiful ability to find every child's strength and interests, and build a strong classroom community based around this knowledge." It was Mrs. Thoren who inspired Tammy to dream about a classroom of her own.

This positive example eventually contributed to Tammy's idea of the ideal classroom. She says, "I try to maintain a mixture of quiet patience, boisterous enthusiasm, and positive outlook, holding the belief that attitude can be just as contagious as the colds notoriously spread throughout elementary schools." Then there is the nitty-gritty; what many in the field refer to as "teacher talk." "Of course, I utilize scientifically research-based curricula, adapting and modifying lessons in order to help all students master the state standards and benchmarks. I use data to drive instruction, create graphs to identify areas of growth and need, employ various methods of assessment to gauge effectiveness of lessons. But I also hope to never get so caught up in the details that I lose sight of the larger purpose of education." Data-driven lessons are one means of achieving best practice, but along with explicit, individualized instruction, Tammy says, students "need to see in their teacher someone who is sincerely passionate about learning, with enthusiasm that is contagious. Kids need real, human role models who love, get sad, become frustrated occasionally, and get so excited about learning that we jump up and down, letting our smiles burst into laughter."

In the age of inclusion and heterogeneous grouping, the position of special education teacher often requires action that can make one unpopular in the staff lounge. If services aren't being delivered and a student's needs aren't being met, the special education teacher must push the issue with the classroom teacher. Hopefully, both sides can be professional, working together for the student's sake. This can happen even when the struggling student isn't classified.

"I have helped to prevent many inappropriate special education referrals, by questioning teachers to find the roots of their students' problems and providing suggestions for intervening and adapting lessons to match the students' needs. Many times these strategies have helped their students succeed in the classroom; sometimes the teacher does try everything possible and the SAT [Student Assistance Team] agrees that a diagnostic evaluation is needed. In any case, I feel that this process has helped all teachers understand that special education is not just a 'dumping ground' for the students with behavior problems or motivation issues that can't seem to make the grade in their classroom."

The student is the responsibility of the regular education teacher with services delivered by the special education teacher as outlined in the individualized education plan. Developing a schoolwide program of inclusion can take a lot of work. Special education teachers like Tammy play an important role, helping teachers and even administrators understand all the intricacies.

"Solutions to the 'inclusion' issue might involve major reorganization of a school's infrastructure and ideologies," Tammy says. "For one thing, administrators need to help create schoolwide schedules that take into consideration students with special needs, and design ways for inclusive classrooms to have the support of a special educator and relevant paraprofessionals as needed. Close inspection of individual education plans would be necessary in order to create schedules that are logistically possible and that meet the needs of all students. This is not an easy task, and in some cases inclusion has seemed impossible because one special education teacher may have fifteen to twenty students on her case load, spread out among ten different classrooms, and she cannot be everywhere at once. Yet the law has no stipulations excusing lack of resources or personnel as reasons not to educate all students in the least restrictive environment." Tammy's point: the answer obviously will differ depending on the circumstances of each school. Let each district, or state, decide for itself: just so long as the issue is being addressed. "Each school and each community require their own solutions, and we need to allow for more local control and management."

Tammy's job can be difficult, but her actions and accomplishments reveal that the secret of her success is sticking to her guns . . . just as she hopes her students will as they grow older. "I believe all students should learn how to remain true to themselves in the midst of a crowd; how to hold on to their original dreams and imagination; how to share our home planet justly with all life; how to respect differences and find commonalities; how to speak with words and actions as well as with silence." In everything she does, Tammy models this for her kids. In less than a decade's time, she has managed to master the art of special education. Not a bad advertisement for alternative certification.

"Miss Tammy has demonstrated an immense desire to continually perfect her job in the rapidly changing field of special education," says Rebecca Archuleta, an assistant teacher at Dulce. "Miss Tammy started with no experience as a special education educator—and has driven herself to become one of the district's finest law-abiding special education educators that they have ever possessed."

For Tammy, teaching isn't just about the legal requirements. It's about the kids, all of the different kinds of students she helps on a daily basis. When asked about her favorite color, a color that might say something about her teaching, Tammy offered an unexpected choice: brown. "A first reaction to this might be, 'You mean your teaching is drab and boring?' But the way I see it, brown is the color of all colors; it is what you get when you mix all your watercolor paints, beautiful for its inclusion of the whole rainbow. Brown is puppy dogs and chocolate and native skin; it is trees and leaves and soil, which gives life to all things." Poetically stated and philosophically sound, a description that could be applied to everything Tammy does. For this reason and so many more, Tammy is modeling for all in her school what an A+ educator is and what every teacher should aim to be.

Tammy says the following factors are necessary: "specialized training for teachers, assistive technology, well-designed individual education plans, adapted materials, training in setting up collaborative learning groups and peer tutoring, inclusion of paraprofessionals or therapists, time for planning and collaboration, sufficient funding, flexibility, and most importantly, proper attitude and a belief in the ability of *all* students to learn and succeed. Research has shown that well-designed inclusive classrooms benefit *all* students."

Pyro Lights the Fire!:
Wyoming's Mark A. Nethercott

— *Advice for Teachers New and Experienced* —

Small, simple, sincere gestures to all students, such as a pat on the back, a smile, a big hello, a compliment, or maybe even a few minutes to just listen without judging, can become dynamic, extraordinary acts that help constructively shape young lives. These are little things that make a big difference in the life of a child.

In 2007 Mark Nethercott was named Wyoming's teacher of the year. He has been teaching for more than two decades and at the time of this big announcement was working toward his National Board Teaching Certification. If the oil industry had been more attractive when he graduated from college, though, Mark never would have set foot in the classroom.

A chemistry, physics, and geology teacher at Afton's Star Valley High School, Mark initially tried using his science degree to get a corporate job and says, "Reflecting upon my life as a teacher and upon the thousands of young lives and minds I've been able to positively influence, I am grateful for a slow job market in the oil industry and a wise professor who led me to a wonderful career in education." Many who have passed through Mark's classroom share that gratitude.

"My nickname at Star Valley High School is 'Pyro,'" he explains. "There is an obvious reason for this pseudo-name of sorts; you see, I teach chemistry using some 'flashy,' but safe, demonstrations. I wish . . . hope . . . to be called 'Pyro' for another reason, however, that being a 'flare' for teaching. I try very hard to 'spark' an interest in my students, so that they do more than go through the motions of learning, and develop the desire to learn on their own. That way I'm not just filling them with knowledge, but they are 'fired up' about self-directed learning." The roots of this nickname, and its congruent philosophy, are made clear when he shares that one of his favorite quotes is William Butler Yeats's "Education is not the filling of a pail, but the lighting of a fire." In that regard, Mark is definitely an educational pyro.

If you examine Mark's teaching through a more pedagogical lens, he uses scaffolding when designing his units and lessons, introducing his students to a general idea before letting them loose to look deeper into the subject matter. "I have approached education with the philosophy that a class should be challenging, yet fun and interesting for every student. I believe that students should have 'LOTS' (lower order thinking skills) before they can have 'HOTS' (higher order thinking skills) and that education should be a hands-on process where students learn by experiencing. Moreover, good self-esteem comes from successful experiences, which are derived from hard work and great effort."

He continues, "I believe educators should go in-depth in our teaching and not just give a topic a superficial once-over. An in-depth study of a topic allows students to use lower-order thinking skills to gain basic knowledge about a subject and also allows the students the opportunity to dig in, use, and master higher-order thinking skills to solve problems, to synthesize, and to evaluate different processes related to the topic."

Mark knows what gets the kids excited, so he tries to provide them with learning they can see and touch. "I strongly believe that students should not only read or hear about a particular topic, but they should also have the opportunity, as much as possible, to experience the concepts we discuss." When studying Newton's laws of motion, for example, he has the kids work on creating a hovercraft in class. When investigating projectile motion, his kids get to launch tennis balls from alcohol cannons in the school's parking lot. And then there are those leftover Halloween pumpkins . . . "These are dropped from the top of the football stadium to measure the acceleration of gravity," he says. "I try to use as many different teaching strategies as possible to touch all students, no matter their learning style.

"One of my favorite activities is to take geology classes on a walk through glacial moraine in Teton National Park and observe glacial effects and features with their eyes and hands, not by looking at a picture in a textbook. It is one thing to talk about an erratic (glacial boulder), another thing to see a picture of an erratic, and yet a whole new world to touch and sit on an erratic."

When asked about his greatest accomplishment as a teacher, Mark doesn't point to one particular student or honor. He says the joy he derives from the job trumps them all and he is given this gift "through the constant day-to-day interactions with my students. I have committed my life to their service and education."

On the one hand, there is the happiness of teaching kids and teaching them well. On the other hand, there are the critical issues facing America's schools. Mark's concern is with the toll of over-testing. "I have spent hundreds of mostly uncompensated hours, outside of my normal class load, working on statewide and districtwide assessments to measure improvement for NCLB (No Child Left Behind). My time would have been better spent preparing lessons, labs, field trips, and developing new teaching skills and strategies." Mark is more than happy to put in this time—he teaches summer school classes and a science "Jumpstart" class for incoming ninth-graders, anyway—just not for all this test prep. "Students literally spend weeks of valuable class time taking assessments to demonstrate proficiency in national, state, and district standards. I believe class time is wasted preparing students for specific assessments so they can score well enough for our school to meet AYP [Adequate Yearly Progress]. I believe students would be better served using this class time improving their skills and learning more in each classroom. . . . The intended benefits of No Child Left Behind are not being realized."

Of a possible solution, Mark says, "I believe NCLB should be modified to give states, school districts, schools, and teachers credit for showing improvement with every student. Schools should be given credit for bringing low-end student scores up 20 percent, 30 percent, or more, even if they were not quite proficient. Likewise, proficient students who improve scores should also count towards a school demonstrating AYP." Mark also has an opinion that might be unpopular with his colleagues. He says, "In order to compensate for weeks of class time missed due to test preparation and testing, I believe the school year should be lengthened by two or three weeks. More federal funding to increase classroom instruction should be provided to meet the mandated requirements of NCLB."

Only an A+ educator would advocate for a longer school year! That, coupled with his "Pyro" nickname, makes one wish they'd had a science teacher like Mark back when they were in school. What could be more fun than alcohol cannons and dropping pumpkins from the bleachers?

In His Own Words

I have helped students know that learning sometimes takes a lot of work, but it can also be fun as well. They have become problem solvers, thinkers, and self-motivated learners.

Celebrating the Strengths:
South Carolina's Ann Marie H. Taylor

Ann Marie H. Taylor was named South Carolina's 2008 teacher of
the year for her good work at Pine Tree Hill Elementary School. At
the time of her award, Ann Marie had been teaching for six years and
had worked with all six grades at her school. In addition to her role as
special educator, she is a teacher trainer and motivational speaker. She
volunteers for the United Way and puts together a team every year
for the American Cancer Society's Relay for Life. Ann Marie is the
founder and president of the Kershaw County Branch of the Council
for Exceptional Children and has won a Habitat for Humanity Award
for her "Classroom Tsunami Project." She served a yearlong residency
at the Center for Educator Recruitment, Retention, and Advancement and is applying for National Board Certification. She certainly
keeps her plate full.

When Ann Marie was named teacher of the year, there were some
perks. She won $25,000 cash and was loaned a 2007 BMW Z-4 road-
ster for one year. For her classroom, she received a SMART board
and a Dell laptop. As a result, Ann Marie says, "My students have
changed through the teacher of the year process. They are so proud
and honored for people to visit, videotape, and interview. It feels great

to be recognized, but more importantly it is empowering to see my students' spirits soar in the process. . . . They are the real winners. I am simply their leader."

One thing Ann Marie is often asked about is her favorite success story. It isn't the BMW. She recalls one student: "I had discovered that the root of Jassmine's difficulty was twofold. First, she saw everything—letters and numbers—upside down and backward. Second, over the course of her education, she had developed learned helplessness. What I also knew about Jassmine was that she was great at several things: she loved to sing and dance, she could learn through song, and she had a great memory. I realized I could teach her skills through songs, and she could learn them easily. Jassmine was also good at conversing with children and adults. She could easily be assessed orally to help her overcome her fear of failure. Jassmine, when treated like a star, thought she was capable of anything. . . . After serving as Jassmine's teacher for the last three years, I saw her read for the very first time last spring. Jassmine is not reading chapter books, but words and print finally make sense to her. She can *read!*" Even those who don't teach can understand the power of this memory for Ann Marie.

One complimentary quote comes from Jassmine's mother, Annie. Of Ann Marie, she writes, "You are like a part of our family. Jassmine loves you so very much. She wakes up in the morning talking about you and she goes to bed at night talking about you. She even wants to ride by your house on our Saturday run to Wal-Mart. My heart is filled with joy as I type this e-mail, Mrs. Taylor. I just wanted to say thank you so much for teaching my little girl. Thank you for taking the time to love her. We love you!"

Ann Marie remembers other students and other success stories, as well. "Kim sitting in her seat instead of crawling on the floor during story time . . . Gary telling me that he did not want to leave my room because I liked him even though he could not read . . . When one of the members of the Kershaw County Teacher of the Year Visitation team said, 'I want to be in your class'. . . The moment Aieshah, who had been in and out of school because she had assaulted several teachers, recited thirty sight words from memory. She learned her alphabet and these sight words in six months' time." One gets the feeling that Ann Marie could go on all day, not just because she has so many success stories, but because these memories are so dear to her.

Ann Marie practices what she preaches and she willingly shares her advice with other teachers during professional development presentations and motivational speeches. It is simple: "Choose to celebrate the strengths in those around you." These words dovetail nicely with one of Ann Marie's favorite quotes: "Children don't control the circumstances under which they are born." These words come from Marian Wright Edelman, a native South Carolinian and the founder of the Children's Defense Fund. It's no surprise to learn that Ann Marie holds a fellow child advocate in such high regard.

Another favorite quote is credited to a former colleague named "Coach B," or Kathy Bradberry, who once said, "Teachers choose the teaching profession for many different reasons. Special education teachers are chosen. They are drawn, some quickly, some gradually, to this world that is different from any other profession. And before they even know it themselves, they are knee deep in emotion. For some it may last only a brief moment, for others it colors every decision they will ever make."

On that topic, Ann Marie says, "Being a special education teacher is my calling. It is my mission in life." She adds, "I believe in them, in spite of their disabilities, and they in turn believe in themselves, as individuals and as a team." Behind her belief in the students is a belief in the philosophy of "servant leadership." This term was coined by Robert Greenleaf and according to Ann Marie, "Servant leadership is a practical philosophy which supports people who choose to serve first and then lead as a way of expanding service to others." This would seem to be a real guiding principal in Ann Marie's professional life.

One of Ann Marie's success stories supports this idea of servant leadership. She recalls, "Jennifer, my classroom paraprofessional, stepped into room 31 at Pine Tree Hill Elementary School planning to be a short-term substitute in my class, never having experienced a special education class before. Three years later, Jennifer is now enrolled in Project CREATE, earning a master's degree in teaching students with disabilities because of the strong community I have helped to build."

"Every parent dreams of having a teacher like this for their child," says John DeFelice, principal of Pine Tree Hill Elementary. "Every teacher longs for a friend like this with whom to share her heart. Every administrator seeks to have a loyal teacher who helps build school unity. Ann Marie Taylor is that teacher."

"I have seen outstanding teachers who did not reach out to their communities in which their students lived. On the other hand, I've seen educators who were extremely active outside their schools but ineffective in their classrooms," says Dr. Herbert M. Berg, superintendent of the Kershaw County School District. "With Ann Marie, you have the total package: a strong instructional teacher who is positively impacting the lives of her students daily in the classroom but who also contributes equally to the community in which she and her students live."

Simply put, Ann Marie tries to do as much as she can for her students. "I offer a welcoming and nurturing environment. I offer insight. I offer a safe haven where my students are loved. I offer them compliments all along the way. I offer them success, sometimes the first success they have ever experienced. I offer them a shoulder to cry on. I offer them a warm heart that is forgiving yet demanding. I offer them discipline, in some cases the only discipline they have ever experienced. I offer a place where they can be themselves, disabilities and all. I offer them a learning environment where they are accepted for who they are and not judged based on their limitations."

That's a lot to try to offer, but when you're an A+ educator, of course you're going to aim high. More often than not, Ann Marie hits her mark.

The Welcome Wagon:
Indiana's Daniel R. Kuznik

In His Own Words

What rewards do you find in teaching? What rewards don't I find in teaching?

In the spring of 2008, the class of 2011 gathered for an assembly. At least that's what one of their favorite teachers thought.

Pike High School Freshman Center Principal Shawn Smith told Daniel Kuznik to bring his math class to the assembly. It was an assembly, Smith explained, about ISTEP, the Indiana Statewide Testing for Educational Progress-Plus. ISTEP is the kind of test every state administers as a result of No Child Left Behind, and no matter how pro-assessment a teacher may be, there is very little chance that Daniel was excited for this assembly. Until he noticed that nobody was discussing ISTEP—and that everybody was looking at him.

Smith was the master of ceremonies at the assembly, only fitting since he was who nominated Daniel for Indiana's teacher of the year. "Mr. Kuznik embodies excellence in the classroom," wrote Smith in that letter. "When you enter his classroom, you witness the teacher who motivates and encourages his students to love math." That letter went to the Indiana Department of Education, which had gathered a committee of its personnel, educational leaders, former Indiana teachers of the year, and community members. After the committee reviewed Daniel's good work, he compared favorably enough to the fifty-two other nominees to be among ten teachers invited for an interview. After meeting Daniel, the committee chose him as the winner.

"Mr. Kuznik clearly has the ability to connect with his students in an important way. The high expectations he sets for his students are a positive example for us all, and we are proud to have him representing us at the national teacher of the year competition." This was the praise shared by Indiana's superintendent of public instruction, Suellen Reed. Pike Township Superintendent Nathaniel Jones said, "Dan is one of those rare educators who understands and embraces the awesome responsibility of educating all children. His strength as a teacher is his ability to connect, interact, and inspire his students to learn."

At the time of his award, Daniel had been teaching for just six years. In that short time, he had been recognized just about every year, in one way or another, for his dedication to excellence in the classroom. He was the district teacher of the year for 2006–07, won the Red ROSE Award for Pike High School, was the district teacher of the year runner-up for 2005–06, was teacher of the year at the Pike High School Freshman Center in 2006, received the Golden Apple Award from the Indianapolis Power & Light Company that same year, and was given the Above and Beyond Award by Superintendent Jones in 2005.

These rewards are nice, but Daniel's favorite reward is the relationship he forms with each student. "The essentials of education are commonly listed as curriculum, instruction, and assessment. I challenge educators to add the essential of relationships. While at first glance it might seem noncurricular, in reality none of the first three essentials can be obtained effectively without forming productive relationships with our students." He adds, "It is not a job that you can just leave on your desk and return the next day; you take it home with you regularly."

These words of wisdom mean even more considering that Daniel has a master's degree in curriculum and instruction. He knows that without the buy-in of the students, all the coursework in the world won't help a teacher to do his or her job. Math teachers love algebra and the good ones know each student is the variable in solving his or her problems.

For understanding how important it is to welcome freshmen to high school, and because he does such a thorough job of modeling excellence for students and staff, Daniel is one of America's brightest teaching stars and, without a doubt, an A+ educator.

Educational Philosophy

Daniel knows how important it is to make freshmen feel welcome when they begin high school. Not only does creating connections help keep the number of dropouts down, it makes the school feel like a safe, friendly place for its students. That's why Daniel leads the Freshman Mentors, a group of approximately 150 upperclassmen who meet once a week to help freshmen with their transition into high school.

Championing Biliteracy:
Delaware's Caridad "Charity" Alonso

────────── *A Defining Moment* ──────────

My mother, a recently retired veteran teacher of over thirty-five years in the Red Clay Consolidated School District and a strong advocate for the Hispanic community, suggested that I pursue a career in the education field. She gave me valuable advice when she stated it was a profession that would allow me to move, touch, and inspire others.

Caridad "Charity" Alonso is a Spanish reading specialist in Wilmington, Delaware, and even her nickname is a lesson in language. In history, too. The word *caridad* is Spanish for "charity," and both words are derived from the Latin *caritas,* which means "generous love." To know Charity Alonso is to know that she is a teacher who gives generous love to her students on a daily basis.

Her principal, Nancy A. Weaver, is well aware of that generosity and the impact it has on everyone at her school. "Mrs. Alonso demonstrates the highest level of professional commitment and competency in her work with students and colleagues. To carry out her professional responsibilities, she gives generously of her valuable time, and her work often extends beyond the school day. She exemplifies the highest standards and is a model of bilingualism for children and adults alike."

As a language teacher, Charity champions a bilingual approach in the classroom. She says, "Biliteracy must become a viable and essential component of educational reform with respect to our underachieving Hispanic population." Her concern is that Hispanics are the fastest growing immigrant population in the country and the poorest achieving academic group. "National concern regarding low literacy achievement levels and disproportionately high educational dropout rates among Hispanic students has given rise to major school reform in the United States. The primary issue at hand is how to rapidly get non–English speakers to become academically successful in English."

There is work to be done, but there are also achievements to be recognized. When asked to describe her favorite, Charity doesn't hesitate. "My greatest teaching accomplishments, after eleven years of teaching, are the cognitive, social, and emotional gains my students make each year, the creation of the Spanish Garden pre-K through first grade foreign language immersion school, and the opportunity to provide professional development in second-language literacy and learning to all teachers in the Red Clay Consolidated School District."

Expanding upon her philosophy of teaching, she says, "I take a constructivist view in that I believe students construct knowledge as they build new ideas upon existing experiences. My students take an active part in class by discussing and sharing their points of view."

Charity's undergrad work was in Spanish and anthropology, but her master's degree is in special education. She realizes that modeling the pursuit of higher education is important for her students. "As an educator, I accept the responsibility of becoming a lifelong learner as new ideas, new technology, and new ways to approach teaching become available. I thrive on opportunities to learn more, reflect upon these, and put them into practice. I also have the challenge as our world becomes more diverse to find ways to meet the educational needs of each student and to make an effort to understand each individual's experiences."

The life Charity has led began to take shape before Charity was even born, as her parents fled Cuba for *los Estados Unidos*. They spoke Spanish at home, so Charity knew almost no English when she started school. Someone told her mother that the best way to help her children was to avoid Spanish at home and speak English exclusively. But Charity's parents had other ideas.

"My mother was an educator, and thank goodness she had a different vision for us," Charity recalls. "She knew we'd learn English by living here, and she wanted us to also maintain our Spanish. I feel enormously fortunate to have come from a bicultural home."

Today she is still guided by that belief and she helps to build literacy in her students by teaching them how to read in their native language first. "The more literate you are in your first language, the more you're able to acquire a second language at a faster rate. . . . That student already has the conceptual knowledge. They have a language to pull from. But if you're illiterate, you not only have to learn the content, but the new language as well."

Charity is not just a language teacher, she is a motivator. To build confidence is key and she asks her students, "Do you know how smart you are to become bilingual and how important that will be in your future?" Charity helps them to make connections between their culture and the culture of Wilmington. She says, "Teaching is not just a 'job' for me. It is my passion. In fact, I know I was born to do this. Each school year, I am dedicated to providing a positive instructional climate where my students feel encouraged, safe and excited to learn."

Day in and day out, Charity creates an environment that allows her students to feel safe and encouraged, excited to learn, and comfortable in their own skin. For her service and generosity, Charity has earned the right to call herself an A+ educator in whatever language she likes.

Educational Philosophy

I strongly believe that every child has learning potential and, with effective instruction, it can be unleashed. In my classroom, I use a variety of instructional strategies in order to address varying learning styles. I isolate each child's learning needs and customize instruction so that every child will benefit. Therefore, no child is ever left behind.

Management Material:
Texas's Paul F. Cain

As baby boomers retire and districts go to great lengths to recruit highly qualified replacements, Paul Cain has some advice for the new teachers: "Find someone you feel you can trust, who is good at their job, and follow them around. Do what they do and don't plan to change the world in your first year of teaching; it can be crushing when you find out it isn't going to happen. You can make some significant contributions to the students and the school, and you're going to be successful, but it's going to take more than fifteen minutes for it to happen. Be patient."

Paul knows what he is talking about. In addition to almost three decades of teaching kids, he has done wonders for those he teaches with. "I've been teaching next door to Paul for twenty-nine years," says Ruth Hansen, the colleague who nominated him for teacher of the year. "He has made a significant difference in *my* development as a teacher. . . . One of the amazing things about Paul Cain is his ability to fit so much into his world."

Way back in the days of disco, *Star Wars,* and Jimmy Carter, Paul was a young, frustrated teacher. After his first year of teaching, he was frustrated enough to quit the job. The assistant principal was able to track him down at his new job at Wyatt's Cafeteria, where he had become a manager trainee. Fortunately, the assistant principal was able to convince Paul to return.

Fast-forward to 2008 and the name "Paul Cain" being announced as the Texas teacher of the year. Paul teaches mathematics and physics at Yselta High School, the same school he once walked away from. In addition, he mentors new teachers and is the math department chair, a seat he had held for eighteen years at the time of his award. Paul coaches Yselta's Quiz Bowl and Academic Decathlon teams and advises the school's University Interscholastic League and National Honor Society. Paul has come a long way since his stint at Wyatt's Cafeteria.

As the department head, Paul made sure that each math teacher instructed at least one section of Algebra I. He wanted them to know what the students in this intro class were like and to make sure the students were getting the basics. Also, "This had the effect of making our entire department responsible to assist our youngest and least motivated students to learn, and it created a pool of teachers willing to share techniques, methodologies, strategies, teaching styles, and information to improve all our teaching skills." A great leader knows how to create a sense of team and, in turn, how to promote teamwork. Perhaps this was a bit of the Army coming out in Paul.

He knows that all is lost if he cannot rely on his colleagues and, to some degree, his students. Therefore, he is sure to focus on their strengths and skills. He has faith in their abilities. "Students already know their problem areas and often are unaware of any strengths they might have," he says. "It is our job as teachers to find those strengths, point them out to the students, and use them to motivate students to participate in the learning process."

All too often, teachers don't give students the credit they deserve. They are aware of their strengths and weaknesses and they are hyper-aware of their surroundings. "Despite complaints from individual teachers that students 'never listen,' I believe they are always listening," Paul says. "They are eavesdropping on adults regularly and take to heart what is said about them. Too many times young people are painfully aware of their shortcomings. . . . These messages come from the adults in their lives and are delivered both in words and actions."

That is why Paul is all about positive, constructive feedback, which he is willing to share with any and all of Yselta's students.

The senior class president, Amanda, says, "When I was a freshman, other kids said if you ever need help, Mr. Cain is the person to come to. Even though he didn't know who I was and I wasn't his student, he still helped me." As a parent, wouldn't it be nice to know that all the teachers are looking out for your child and not just those on his or her course load? And as a parent, wouldn't it be nice to know there were positive messages being sent your child's way, rather than negative?

"A lot of teachers just focus on grades; he praises effort," says Patricia, a former student and the National Honor Society president. "He doesn't add on extra pressure. He makes it a comfortable atmosphere in the classroom. He'll work with you after school or in the morning. He'll work with your schedule." The bottom line is, he'll work.

For all the work he does and all the work he's done, rather than being a heckuva cafeteria manager Paul Cain is an A+ educator.

Educational Philosophy

When I started teaching, kids didn't always want to be in your class but they wanted to be on campus, because that's where they all hung out. . . . It was the place to be to meet friends and socialize as well as learn. We now must compete for the students' attention, and this is not easy. With the introduction of technology, they can communicate classroom to classroom, city to city. They don't need to be in the same physical location. We've lost that edge. We need to find another edge to get them to come to school and be interested in being there.

From Father to Son:
Utah's Hal W. Adams

—————— *Compliments to the Teacher* ——————

In the past five years, "we've been to state championships three times and runner-up twice in debate," Grand County High School Principal Stephen Hren says of the school debate team which Hal coaches. "We go to invitation-only tournaments. We have gone to Harvard, Stanford, Arizona State."

Hal Adams comes from a long line of teachers. The first Adams to teach was his great-great-grandfather. More recently, there was Clemont Adams, Hal's father, who taught for thirty-seven years. "There's no greater happiness than being able to lift other people," Hal says, "to be able to serve and lift other people. I remember my dad telling me a long time ago (about) the joy of seeing one of your students succeeding."

When Hal was a boy, though, school wasn't always a happy place for him. He had a speech impediment that left him shy and, all too often, questioning his abilities. He recalls that teachers and coaches helped him overcome the impediment. They even invited him to participate on the school debate team. Nowadays, Hal is the one who does the inviting, and approximately 25 percent of Grand County's five hundred students participate. Hal isn't exclusive when it comes to extending these invitations.

"I'd rather it be known as a place that includes people than wins," he says.

Hal has shown that there is no risk too great for him by also taking on the role of school driving instructor. All of these things added up to statewide recognition when, in 2008, he was named Utah's teacher of the year. At the time of this award, Hal had been debating and driving with students for seventeen years.

Hal began his career on the Navajo Nation Reservation in Arizona and has taught students of every age "but kindergarten and second grade," he says. When he won the teacher of the year award, Hal said, "This night is probably the night I've felt my whole life. It's living up to the heritage I have as a teacher." On that same night, he recalled the words of a Native American elder, spoken to him after winning an earlier award: "This is just a moment in passing. Go home and be a good teacher." And he has followed that advice.

Hal was more than happy to celebrate his success and then get back to work. He says, "As educators, we sometimes are a little shy about tooting our own horn. We have done so much with so little for so long, we're afraid that they'll expect us to do everything with nothing." This quote, however, had more to do with celebrating public education than individual achievement.

Because Grand County High School is in Moab, Hal defends not just public education, but public education in rural locales. Arguing against vouchers, he says, "Our rural communities are 100, 200, even 300 miles from a private school. . . . In all those years, our schools in rural Utah have played a unique role; they are often the social and cultural centers of our communities." He adds, "School pride and community pride are synonymous." Aptly and convincingly, Hal certainly knows how to put his debate skills to use, especially when the stakes are so high, such as a recent ballot initiative to support school budgets.

While giving to the students, Hal has received much in return. "My greatest contributions in education have been in extending the classroom learning to real-life opportunities. My teaching has rewarded me in a very special way as I have served others and tried to make a difference in shaping their lives. My own life has been refined. I have developed a love of learning, a special sense of humor, my appreciation of beauty and diversity, gratitude and caring have replaced greed and selfishness. I love life." Although there will always be problems in schools to deal with, Hal sounds like a man happy to carry on the family tradition. He sounds like a teacher who has no problem heeding the elder's advice, keeping his ego in check while tending to his classroom. These are just some of the reasons why Hal is a true A+ educator.

In His Own Words

I am so grateful to be a teacher. It is the most noble of all callings.

A Really Good Choice:
Pennsylvania's Lois J. Rebich

Today Lois Rebich is a special education teacher, and her position at Pittsburgh's Ross Elementary School is listed as "instructional support," which implies that Lois supports both students and staff. Whatever gaps need to be filled, she's there to fill them. Be it a kindergarten activity or a sixth-grade test, Lois's job is to help.

Lois might be a gap-filler, but she isn't a lifer. The first part of her professional career was not spent in schools. Act I saw her punching the clock at Heinz and then at Rockwell International. Of the switch to teaching, she says, "It was a love affair with the classroom I hadn't expected. The good news is, I still have that love affair with the classroom."

There is enough love and talent there to have earned her the honor of Pennsylvania Teacher of the Year in 2007. She got there by challenging her students, her colleagues, and herself. "When I moved from the boardroom to the classroom," she recalls, "my goals and philosophy were clear; to instill in my students the qualities and zeal necessary to promote personal growth, a thirst for knowledge, and to take on the responsibility and the opportunity to compete in our global society. To that end, I challenge my students to be lifelong learners, aim high, be inquisitive, and always do their best."

These ideas grew out of what she'd experienced in the business world for all that time. "Having worked many years in corporate America before entering the field of education, it was my privilege to be employed by Fortune 500 firms who were recognized as outstanding in their sectors. Without exception, the overall success of those companies originated from the skill, knowledge, enthusiasm, and innovation of its employees." What Lois aims to do is cultivate these four traits in those around her. Apparently, she has done so with the practiced touch of a diplomat. After the staff and students learned that one of their favorite teachers was the best in the state, the compliments rained down. A student named Mitchell says, "Whenever something bad happens, I go to her. She's helped me a lot. She helps me with tests and quizzes and whatever I need. Giving her that award was a really good choice." A good choice, indeed.

Lois graduated from the University of Pittsburgh with two bachelor's degrees, one in mathematics and the other in economics. Then there was a master's degree in business administration. Life slowed down a little when she had children, then picked up again when she decided to get the teaching certification needed to run a day care center.

After Act II of Lois's life got under way, she worked for ten years as a regular education teacher in first, second, and third grades. Then she became her school's instructional support teacher, which was when Lois experienced the defining moment of her professional life. Lois remembers a former student, a sixth-grader with Tourette's syndrome. Her approach, for the benefit of the student and his classmates, was to make them aware of the boy's strengths. Lois wanted them to see beyond the disability, to see all he had to offer. Fortunately, these strengths were in two areas widely respected by those classmates: computers and a sense of humor. By the end of the year, Lois's efforts had paid off. The other students learned to accept the boy, and she says, "The learning that took place that year, for all of us, exceeded any measure of AYP [Adequate Yearly Progress], yet it could not be assessed with paper and pencil or quantified by a grade." Lois knows what lies at the heart of any good school, and it isn't test scores. It is people.

Lois utilizes a shared inquiry approach, which she finds empowering for those she works with. "My role as a facilitator offers guidance in the process but allows the discovery of knowledge to reside with the individual, the partners, the teams, or the class as a whole," she explains.

"Mrs. Rebich is a leader and a role model to her colleagues and her students at Ross Elementary School," Representative Jason Altmire shared after she had received her award. "She has excelled by coordinating her efforts with parents, teachers, administrators, and other students."

"Great teaching," Lois says, "is brimming with energy, excitement, and passion. It's where students are motivated, teachers are vibrant, and learning is interactive. Do not confuse excellence with perfection; remind your students that failure is just another opportunity to try again." One cannot survive as a special education teacher without a great sense of humility. In addition, every perceived failure must not only be turned into a teachable moment, it must be made to look like a positive. The learners in Lois's charge run the risk of fragile self-esteem, and to keep these kids feeling good about school, and themselves, the lesson of "that's why they make pencils with erasers" must be delivered professionally and convincingly.

One reason many children have low self-esteem is bullying. Students classified in one of the special education categories tend to be more prone to bullying than other kids, and perhaps this is why Lois is so aware of the dangers. She calls this the biggest issue facing schools today. "Bullying has been a common occurrence in schools for decades, yet with the increase of school violence and shootings, it has become a topic widely addressed by parents, educators, and the media. The attitudes and opinions of all involved conclude that bullying is no longer being accepted as a normal part of growing up." That said, there is still work to be done. Lois offers, "Both prevention and intervention are the keys to addressing bullying. In my district, I work with students at the classroom level to role-play situations and possible strategies to use in refusing or reporting the bully. I encourage and train students in assertive behavior techniques as well as conflict resolution and peer mediation skills." "Figure it out" is a phrase commonly used in day care centers as little people learn their first lesson in conflict resolution. Lois really knows how to tap into her experiences and to empower her students.

After the teacher of the year announcement, Ross Principal Barbara Weber Mellett said, "We are delighted as a school and as a staff. You could not ask for a more dedicated professional committed to children and meeting their needs." You could not ask for a more dedicated, more professional, more committed teacher. That is why Lois was a good businesswoman but is now an A+ educator.

A Defining Moment

After Lois received her award, a student asked Lois what she'd won. "So I told him about the SMART board and projector for the classroom, the laptop computer, books, and school supplies, and I could see he was not very impressed. Then I told him the nice people from Hershey Corporation gave me a huge five-pound Hershey chocolate bar—that brought a smile to his face."

Colonel Wagon Train:
California's Chauncey Veatch

On April 24, 2002, President George W. Bush named Chauncey Veatch the fifty-second National Teacher of the Year. Chauncey, a social science teacher at California's Coachella Valley High School, had managed to excel in a second career.

Chauncey is a graduate of the American High School in Frankfurt, Germany. He earned his bachelor's degree from the University of the Pacific and a law degree from the University of Notre Dame. Chauncey is also a graduate of the U.S. Army Command and General Staff College at Fort Leavenworth, Kansas, and in his twenty-two years of service, he was stationed in Spain, Costa Rica, Panama, El Salvador, Paraguay, and Peru. Learning Spanish served him well while he served and would once again, after he retired from the military and decided to teach.

Ninety-nine percent of Coachella's students are Hispanic and many are English-language learners. Typically one-third of his students come to him with an individualized education plan, meaning that they receive special education services. None of this phases him, though. "Most of my students come from families of modest economic means, but their parents have the same dreams for them as parents everywhere."

As someone who has seen the world and understands the importance of managing one's finances, Chauncey has dedicated hours of time to teaching his kids basic money skills. "We use the Visa Practical Money Skills Program in my high school economics classes for a variety of purposes. We use it to work with family and personal budgets. We use it to understand the intricacies of the global economy. They are easily aligned to our state standards. They also serve as a potent supplement to our work with our ELL (English-language learners) students."

Chauncey wants to have an impact on students' lives and be involved with the community around Coachella, even if it means working on the weekends. Along with the students, he has passed out health care–related leaflets in migrant labor camps, and he developed a buddy program, focused on literacy, with third-graders at two local elementary schools. He was able to reestablish the California Cadet Corps, a leadership- and citizenship-development program for juniors and seniors and includes lessons on the military and the role of the armed forces in a democracy. Not only has Chauncey's first career benefited his students, but it also has enabled him to bring other retired officers into the classroom. He is an active member in the Troops to Teachers Program, and Eric Combs, also featured in this book as a teacher of the year from Ohio, got into teaching as a result of this program.

Chauncey doesn't fit the stereotypical description of a military man. Listen to Richard Alvarez, former Coachella Valley High School principal, describe him. "There is no doubt in my mind, heart, and soul that when I met Chauncey Veatch, I met an individual whom I knew I was going to call my friend. Always kind and courteous, he has a sincere concern for the children of our community and a positive attitude. Believing our students can succeed is not a desire or a facade but is actually something he lives. This caring can be seen in his eyes, heard in his voice, felt in his presence, and mostly seen in his actions."

Considering this was a job Chauncey took on later in life, words can hardly describe the enormity of his achievement. Seven years after entering the classroom, seven years after leaving one profession for another, he was celebrated as tops in his field.

In addition to teaching grades nine through twelve, Chauncey has served on the Federal Task Force on Homelessness and Severe Mental Illness, the National Advisory Council on Drug and Alcohol Abuse, and the Blue Ribbon Commission on the Year of Languages. He is the College Board's international visiting scholar, serves on Visa USA's Educator Advisory Council, and is an author and academic adviser in the development of students' critical language and reading skills for Scholastic's Zip Zoom English, Read 180, and RED programs. He was named international ambassador for education by *La Prensa Hispana* and is part of the PTA's National Outreach program to help African American, Hispanic American, and Native American students. He is one of those teachers who really know how to tap into all available resources.

"I tell my students," Chauncey says, "that our class is like a wagon train heading out across this great expanse of learning to reach our goal: an education. No one will be thrown overboard; no one will be left behind. Together we are all going to get there." Chauncey also likes to describe himself as "a dream-maker for my students, not a dream-breaker."

Many of Chauncey's students lead a nomadic life. Some might not even be citizens. In Chauncey's part of the world, migrant workers are common. One migrant student named Luiz says, "I work with my family around Bakersfield until November. But Mr. Veatch saved me a place in his class and spent hours with me helping me to catch up. He does this for all of his migrant students."

What is it that motivates Chauncey to make sure that everyone feels they belong? Why is it that he is willing to save seats for students who are rarely present? One answer is that only these types of gestures will help with dropout prevention. Another is that "literacy leads to success in school, success in a career, and success in life. A literate person will have more options in life and a greater likelihood of becoming a lifetime learner."

Luiz adds, "His goal for us is literacy, but he gives us all much more. Mr. Veatch sets high standards and helps us to reach them, and helps us achieve our dreams. My dream is to one day be an ambassador for the United States. Maybe I can be an ambassador to one of the countries I read about in a big book (about European royal palaces) that Mr. Veatch gave me." After a few years in the classroom, Chauncey knew he was in the business of dreams. "To dream is to be filled with hope. I know this because I see the faces of hope daily."

Colonel Chauncey Veatch is an inspiration to his students, as well as other teachers learning how to succeed in their second career. He is an A+ American and an A+ educator.

Educational Philosophy

Since becoming a teacher in 1995, Chauncey has also taught English as a second language, as well as a citizenship class, as a part of the Adult Education School. This is an extension of the Coachella Valley Unified School District and is attended by many of the parents of those kids he teaches during the day.

A Mentor and Master Teacher:
Washington's Andrea Peterson

In 2007 a kindergarten teacher from Granite Falls, Washington, thrilled everyone at Monte Cristo Elementary School when she was named the state's teacher of the year. There was a symphony of joy when, a few months later, the Council of Chief State School Officers announced that Andrea Peterson was also National Teacher of the Year.

Andrea was born in Canada and became an American citizen in 2004, and some might say her choice to teach music was all in the family. Her father was a physical education teacher who became a special education teacher, and Andrea was able to visit an older brother at college while he studied music education. She pursued a degree in education at the University of Washington and immediately began to establish a reputation of excellence. Andrea was the first National Board Certified Teacher in early and middle childhood music in the state of Washington.

"Music is an amazing tool to unlock students' potential," she says. "The most visible benefit from their success in music is their increased confidence and self-esteem."

One standout area for Andrea is her effort to create crosscurricular units. "It is truly exciting to see how my music teaching can transfer back to other classrooms," she says with pride. In facilitating multidisciplinary units with various social studies teachers, Andrea has used her musical talents to honor Dr. Martin Luther King Jr., as well as veterans. One of the most popular units she has her kids do every year is a performance for the community of a musical based on a book from their English class. One recent show was S. E. Hinton's *The Outsiders.*

"This is not just singing, but playing instruments, reading music, understanding fractions, performance behavior, and so much more. Many of these skills have transferred into other areas of their lives," says Sarah Edwards, an obviously pleased parent.

Andrea's colleagues are pleased, as well. "Through Andrea's efforts these kids have helped to put Granite Falls, Washington, on the map for musical talents," says Debra Rose Howell. "Parents, staff, and community members continue to be in awe of what she is able to bring forth from the children." Joel Thaut, superintendent of Granite Falls School District, adds, "Mrs. Peterson's music program is not a complement to our basic education program; it is an integral part of it."

Andrea is obviously aware of the big picture. In addition to supplementing the efforts of the English and social studies teachers, she has worked with the math teachers. "I have had the opportunity to teach symmetry, geometrical sense, inference, and prediction. Some of these lessons have had nothing to do with music but have had everything to do with teaching in a way that's best for kids." She says, "I am a teacher first, music is my curriculum."

Andrea expands upon her philosophy. "Teaching is an amazingly complex combination of science and art. Scientifically, teachers must know how to teach to students' individual learning styles, breaking down the components of knowledge and skill into attainable pieces. Artistically, teachers must be able to inspire their students to excellence, showing them a world that is bigger than their own. I believe I am an outstanding teacher because I am balancing the art and science of teaching."

What Andrea hopes to see is outstanding schools, populated by other outstanding teachers educating outstanding students. She says, "All too often, our society accepts mediocrity as satisfactory. In and out of school, we tell children that it is acceptable to do things incorrectly, as long as they feel good about themselves. The intrinsic problem, of course, is that human beings never feel good about themselves unless they are achieving." Sometimes people need to be challenged, just so long as it is in a supportive manner.

As a National Board Certified teacher, Andrea has the opportunity to also support colleagues working toward their own certification. "Because I was the only certified elementary music specialist in the state, I began mentoring new music candidates in Washington and Idaho. From reading their portfolio entries, to working with them personally, I truly enjoy the role of mentor. I am also an active recruiter of new candidates for the National Board." This goes along with what Andrea sees as *the* critical issue facing schools today, improving the quality of teachers. "We teachers are not unlike our students. We too are comfortably unaware of our lack of knowledge. Our teaching limitations must be revealed through traditional principal observations, personal reflective analysis of our teaching (through videotape or other means), and/or analysis of test scores (always bearing in mind socioeconomic differences)." As she sees it, the best way to combat mediocre teaching is to assign a master teacher as a mentor. This is why she puts in all that extra time.

"Most teachers want to succeed. They entered the profession with a desire to help children," she says. "They simply need to be shown, in manageable sequences, how to achieve this goal."

For showing teachers how to teach as best they can, for showing music students how important their academics are, Andrea is a trailblazer. She is a teacher first and a music teacher second. She is truly an A+ educator.

A Defining Moment

As a music teacher, Andrea has to do a fair amount of fund-raising to buy new instruments. To date, she has raised more than $55,000, which far surpassed her original goal.

A Man of Multiple Intelligences:
Rhode Island's George Edwin Goodfellow

In His Own Words

I teach. It's what I do. And I'm not done yet. I don't think I'll ever be.

It took George Goodfellow more than two decades to discover the educational philosophy he'd always been looking for. He has spent almost twenty years now perfecting it within his classroom and chemistry lab.

In 2008 George was named Rhode Island's teacher of the year, seventeen years after running across Howard Gardner's theory of multiple intelligences. Gardner, a Harvard psychologist, gave proponents of individualized instruction all the ammunition they would ever need when he laid out nine areas of student strength and stated that every person has at least one of these strengths, or "intelligences." As the presence of special education grew, Gardner's theory was particularly useful to classroom teachers trying to meet the needs of all their students—teachers like George.

"Once you prove to them that they are not inferior, just different," he says, beaming, "they can soar in ways you never expected." And George recalls, "When I first heard about this research, I felt like I had spent twenty-two years in the classroom blowing it." Ever since, he's been working hard to show how often this theory can be applied.

George is an eleventh-grade chemistry teacher at Scituate High School in North Scituate, Rhode Island. After a Sigma Psi award, an Outstanding Inspirational Teacher Award from Clarkson University, and three nominations for Disney Teacher of the Year, George finally got his due. And people were ecstatic.

In a newspaper editorial, George's sister, Jan Oliveira, wrote, "I am writing this with so much pride for our whole family. I know I can speak for all of them. Our husband, son, father, brother, and friend George Goodfellow was just named Teacher of the Year 2008 for Rhode Island. This is a man who has spent his whole adult life giving to young people and extending himself always. . . . With what we pay our teachers, we are blessed when we have teachers like my brother—teachers who don't just show up, teachers who teach all the lessons we want our young adults to learn and to use in life."

For George it has long been a family affair. His wife, Cindy, is a retired teacher and volunteers in his classroom every day. Together they developed a motto: "Wrap the student around the curriculum, not the curriculum around the student." When George learned that as part of his teacher of the year award he was invited to attend a meeting of all state teachers of the year, he said he would attend only if Cindy could attend, as well. They went together.

At the ceremony in Rhode Island, Patrick A. Guida, vice chair of the state Board of Regents for Elementary and Secondary Education, said, "What I most admire about Mr. Goodfellow is his innovation and talent in making learning fun. If we are to make American public education superior globally, we will need more such innovation and talent in refocusing our popular culture on quality education."

While making his lessons enjoyable, George does not sacrifice quality or curricular relevance. Working with juniors means that college—or at least graduation—is just around the corner. He knows that real success is not marked by fun or off-the-charts test scores, but by leading kids down their road to success.

"Many of his students have gone on not only to college, but to graduate school in chemistry and engineering," said Peter McWalters, Rhode Island commissioner of Elementary and Secondary Education, at the ceremony. "But his finest accomplishment, he says, is to teach all of his students to have pride in themselves and their accomplishments and to instill in them the joy of learning. He will represent his profession well as Teacher of the Year."

"With thirty-nine years of classroom experience," said Governor Donald L. Carcieri at the ceremony, "George Goodfellow is a veteran teacher who sets high standards and challenges his students. He not only makes science relevant to students' lives, but he also makes learning fun."

George enjoyed meeting the governor and even took advantage of the opportunity to describe how public education might be improved in the state. George told Carcieri, "Governor, if you cut class size in half, or put two professionals in every classroom, you'll get it done."

One of the quickest ways to make an impact on people is with memorable quotes, and George has quite a few. Among his favorite are:

"In a service occupation, the key to productivity is morale."

"One can lead a horse to water but he will drink only if he is thirsty and believes that the water is safe."

"Children do not say what they believe. They say what works. For what they will truly believe is still in its formative stage."

"Learning occurs at the moment of wonder."

"Content rigor occurs after content inspiration."

Although all of these could be used in a conversation with a student or a colleague, this last quote seems to be especially relevant to life as a new teacher. "If you wish to build a ship, do not give directions and technical advice to others. Rather, show them the wonder and adventure of the open ocean." Thirty-nine years is a long time, but not so long that George has forgotten his first year of teaching. It was then, way back in 1968, that he actually had his greatest accomplishment. He remembers, "In year number one I had a student, Diane, who never showed up to class for the entire first quarter. When I met her I learned that she had been a runaway and the courts ordered her back to school. Her F of the first quarter turned into an A for the year because she came to me every spare minute to learn what she needed to succeed. I realized that it is the personal relevance that causes content rigor to be achieved. We had to show her her worth and then she could conquer any academic or personal problem. It was then that I learned the function of a teacher and the lifelong effect our position creates in students."

Considering that he knows what it takes to bring out the best in his students, not to mention that he insisted on taking his coteacher along to Dallas for that meeting of the minds, of course George is an A+ educator. After all, he's probably forgotten more about good teaching than most other A+ educators know.

Educational Philosophy

George believes that students progress because of three mind-sets: "(1) They are *humble* enough to see the importance of possible future learning, (2) they believe in their ability to accomplish this learning, and (3) they are inspired about the possibility that they will eventually be successful." He says he tries to keep this in mind with every lesson plan he writes.

A Teacher's Purpose, A Child's Future:
Nevada's Melanie Teemant

In Her Own Words

In my classroom, the students never know what is up my sleeve.

Melanie Teemant has grown up to become a top-notch teacher, and the seed was planted back when she was in school. "My high school teachers fueled the teaching spark by regularly pointing out that I had a special way of working with groups of people and getting results. To this day, I thrive when I see other people achieving things they once thought were impossible."

From the student perspective, a boy named Max says, "She doesn't really single anybody out or play favorites. She's helpful to everybody."

For Melanie, the single most helpful thing she does is refuse to lower the bar of expectations, even for disabled students. She has high expectations and will do whatever it takes to help her kids live up to them.

"The students in my class know that *can't* is not an option. I start the year instilling a spirit of perseverance in them. I teach them that if there is a wall in their way, they can go around it, over it, under it, or through it, but they can never be stopped by it. I reinforce that as human beings we have to be resourceful and willing to overcome the obstacles we face to get the life we ultimately want."

It was this level of dedication, this unique fighting spirit, that helped Melanie to earn top honors in Nevada as 2007 teacher of the year. At this recognition, everyone at Bob Miller Middle School, where Melanie teaches seventh grade, rejoiced. Although Melanie has a passion for her subject, reading isn't foremost on her mind when the day begins. "I try to remember each day that what I teach is not as important as how I teach or who I teach." She adds, "Because each child is distinct, it requires an approach that reminds them of that. In the classroom, there are brief, enlightening encounters that can become teachable moments, defining a child's future and a teacher's purpose. As a guardian of their human potential, I search for those defining moments in the classroom and use them to help them be the best they can possibly be."

To tap into their potential, Melanie designed a unit she calls her crowning achievement. It is a multidisciplinary unit that consists of a research project *and* a musical production. The students spend a couple of months on this unit, called "Dancing Through the Decades." At the end, the community is invited in to see what Melanie's students have come up with. "We get more than one thousand people," she says, beaming. "It's standing room only. Even the principal performs. Last year the administration dressed up as the Beatles."

As the students work on the "Dancing Through the Decades" unit, they design PowerPoint slides, read from primary sources about things like the first walk on the moon, put together a film about each decade, dance out in the courtyard, write and edit essays, or listen to music from the era. It has been proven that multidisciplinary units of this nature go a long way toward increasing student engagement.

Melanie recalls, "Last week I stopped to talk to a boy who was my student last year. I said, 'It's 3:30, Matt, don't you want to go home?' His reply was all I needed to hear. He said, 'I love school, Mrs. Teemant. Ever since I was in your class, this is my favorite place to be.' I have the power to provide a safe environment and a stimulating curriculum for learning that counteracts absenteeism."

People also like to learn about themselves, and Melanie finds ways to work that into her curriculum, especially with the "Dancing Through the Decades" unit. "We find interesting information that will connect us to our past. . . . I stimulate them to think and learn more than they thought was possible, but I also challenge them to find out about who they are and how they can be a better individual by being at school each day."

In addition to teaching reading, Melanie advises the student council, as well as the guitar and scrapbooking clubs. In everything she does, in every interaction she has with students, she hopes to plant a seed that will then spread to others. "My greatest contribution to education is teaching my students that once you've learned something, you need to use it and share that knowledge to become a better person."

Accountability and high expectations go hand-in-hand, and both are evident in Melanie's approach to teaching. "Another important part of my teaching philosophy is that high expectations should not only be directed toward students," she says. "Teachers must also hold themselves as accountable for high-quality teaching as they hold students for high-quality learning performances. Every day I have the opportunity to model my philosophy in my own actions." Riffing further on the subject, she gives her fellow teachers some advice: "Keep it passionate and teach from the heart!"

Melanie knows some educators have lost their enthusiasm. This doesn't mean they should retire, it means they should recharge. "I would advise them to remember why they chose teaching in the first place. We do not go into the teaching profession for the money or the rewards, we do it because we have a passion for teaching children and changing lives."

For her professionalism and dedication, Melanie was invited to attend President George W. Bush's State of the Union address, but she would love to be invited to more meaningful conversations. In a press conference in Senator Harry Reid's office, she stated, "If we do not invite teachers to the table every time we make decisions about the American classroom, we will never close the gap completely because they are the experts that can provide the relevant information that will take us into twenty-first-century teaching and learning where our students can compete with the rest of the world and still achieve on a national level."

Just as Melanie's teachers delivered her to the classroom to serve as a teacher, she is working hard to deliver her students to the eighth grade, then to high school, and then to the world beyond: that twenty-first-century world. Only an A+ educator would have such vision, and only an A+ educator would know that to learn is to dance and that sometimes to dance is to learn.

Educational Philosophy

We can no longer standardize human beings and call it success. We must cherish our differences, abilities, and work to be the very best we can. In this way, we will not leave our country behind.

Moved by Michael, Moved by Katrina: Illinois's Ruth E. Meissen

Nylant's loss was Harlem Middle School's gain. After working for several years as the vice president of the Northern Illinois Advertising Council and as the art director of Nylant, a toy company, Ruth Meissen took a few years off to raise her children. When she was ready to return to work, though, it was not to Nylant or to the advertising council. Instead, she listened to the advice of a seven-year-old—her son, Michael—who told her she should be an art teacher.

"I thought that was the most insane thing I had heard," says a reminiscent and reflective Ruth, laughing.

In 1994 that advice came to fruition as she became a seventh- and eighth-grade art teacher. Fourteen years later, Ruth had garnered enough notice, earned enough respect, and touched enough lives to be named Illinois Teacher of the Year. This time, mother didn't know best.

"It's surprising what that suggestion has become," says Michael. "But in the same sense, it's not that surprising."

Recalling her life in business, Ruth says, "The intensity of my previous career made the potential chaos of a classroom full of active students seem easily manageable. But most of all, being able to share my artistic knowledge and love for creating artwork with students was absolutely exhilarating."

According to special education teacher Mary Beth Westin, the ability to manage means that Ruth can contribute outside of her classroom, as well. "She'll do anything you ask her. She has boundless energy."

When Hurricane Katrina struck, it was time to put that boundless energy to use. Her efforts came as a result of seeing a Spike Lee documentary about that natural disaster. She remembers wondering, "How could this happen in my America?" After watching the documentary, *When the Levees Broke,* Ruth decided to ask her students if they would like to help out. "Everything that was paper was lost. Everything that was wood was rotted," she recalls. "Everything metal was rusted."

The students collected books and learning materials, as well as money. Principal John Cusimano says, "Her efforts have not only helped the Hynes staff and students, but allowed our staff and students to unify in an effort to reach out to others."

Hynes Elementary School in New Orleans was hit particularly hard. Before Hurricane Katrina, Hynes had been home to 830 students and 50 teachers. After Katrina, there were only 410 students and 35 teachers and staff. Hynes Assistant Principal Shawn Persick says, "It's just unbelievable. I try not to get choked up. It's for the kindness of strangers that makes you really stop and think, 'we can do things.'"

"I know the type of person that Ruth is, and it's easy to support her," says Cusimano. "It was something that I knew would be done the right way with Ruth being in charge."

Although it doesn't compare to what the folks at Hynes had to endure, life at Harlem Middle School in Loves Park, Illinois, had been pretty tough leading up to Ruth's teacher of the year announcement. The district had recently suffered through a teachers' strike that delayed the start of school after failed contract negotiations. Fortunately, good news goes a long way toward healing.

"Ruth's passion and commitment to the arts, coupled with her dedication to community service, makes her an excellent representative of teachers throughout the state," says Christopher A. Koch, state superintendent of education. "What Ruth has accomplished within the classroom, the school, and the community as a whole is truly impressive."

"She cared about the students," adds Frankie, a former student. "If I had late work from another class, she would help me."

Tyler, another former student, gives the praise all teachers want to hear. "You can talk to her about regular stuff."

Ann Muraro, state coordinator for the teacher of the year award, shared words short and sweet: "She has got it all."

Ruth was selected from among 170 nominees for her award. Amidst all those standout teachers, Ruth was head and shoulders above the rest. Perhaps it was the care she demonstrated for others during their time of need. Perhaps it was her willingness to talk to kids and to even help them when struggling in somebody else's class. Whatever the reason, the educational leaders in Illinois were wise to recognize that Ruth Meissen is an A+ educator.

—— *Advice for Teachers New and Experienced* ——
As part of her teacher of the year duties, Ruth traveled around the state, speaking to her fellow teachers. Ever the motivational speaker, the theme of her talks was "Do the most you can do."

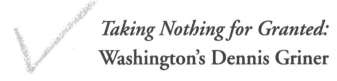

Taking Nothing for Granted:
Washington's Dennis Griner

It might not be turning water into wine, but when a grant writer, administrator, or teacher can bring extra money into a school, that infusion of funding is the educational version of a miracle. All schools could use a little more in the coffers, especially public schools.

Dennis Griner is a public school teacher whose father was an eighth-grade dropout. Dennis went on to be the only person in his family to graduate from college, and now he teaches social studies to juniors and seniors at Garfield-Palouse High School. Although he has been teaching for more than thirty years, Dennis is showing no signs of slowing down. He is still willing to give driving lessons to students and to negotiate contracts for his union. He works with his fellow teachers to help them improve their craft, and he works to bring more technology into Garfield-Palouse. This is a man who cares about his school and his profession as a whole.

Dennis indisputably brings a lot to the table as a teacher, and the funding he has procured from various organizations has enhanced his teaching ability. "I have successfully written numerous grants that have funded computers, cameras, scanners, printers, and digital cameras," he says. For example, his current world issues class is using grant money for a regional water aquifer study. "My students are compiling information for a report to the school board in December on water conservation/use, as the school is one of the largest water users in the community. My students worked with the executive director of the regional water board from the University of Idaho, a geology professor from Washington State University who is responsible for much of the research on this topic, and the City of Palouse water manager. My students gathered data from graduate research papers, government publications, community water records, and the Internet. Using digital cameras, scanners, and digital graphics software, they are preparing a report to be presented to the school board in December. Each student has an assigned support role and a speaking role in the presentation. In addition to the oral presentation, a report in DVD format is being prepared, as well as an official written report that will document their research procedures. When my students complete projects such as the one described, I am confident that learning has taken place because they have been challenged to go beyond their level of knowledge and skill." When the students did their review, no doubt the organization that helped fund this work was pleased.

Dennis's colleagues and administrative team must also be pleased Authentic learning does much to increase student engagement, and by writing the grant, planning the unit, assigning appropriate roles to the students, and seeing the project through, Dennis has shown that he is a teacher and not just a grant writer. He says, "Student 'buy-in' was accomplished through providing a 'real-life' situation that had an actual purpose and value in the community in which they live. I am confident that by taking learning into the community, a positive environment can be created that results in a win-win situation for students and the teacher."

Dennis is driven by the desire to promote the good work done in America's public schools and to further improve upon all that good. He says, "Free public education has been the foundation upon which this nation grew to become the leading industrialized nation in the world. Now its very future is being put in question. How can that be? Equal opportunity is the banner that needs to be flown over every public school." Dennis sounds remorseful, though, as he says, "Finally, the rising expectations upon the public school system may bring it down by the sheer weight of the duties it is expected to fulfill." Specifically, he is concerned about "(1) the lack of confidence by the general public that the public education system can carry out its mission to educate our children, (2) the public's perception that the system is beyond repair, (3) the low esteem that the profession of teaching holds in the professional and business world, (4) the lack of will to find the funding to timely restructure the system, attract highly competent teachers, provide tools necessary for the classroom, and maintain the superstructure." The way he sees it, "We have the resources and we have the finances but we need commitment now. We cannot wait for a booming economy. We cannot wait for full employment. We cannot wait for the stock market to reach new record highs. Children need us now as their voice and as their champions. . . . If we, the American people, government officials, and especially teachers do not boldly and confidently step forward to speak out as well as take action, it will be to the detriment of our children."

Since 2004 Dennis has enjoyed a more public platform for speaking his mind. That year he was named Washington's teacher of the year and was a finalist for National Teacher of the Year. In addition to memberships in several historical organizations, Dennis is involved with mentoring new teachers and with integrating technology into the school. Before receiving his teacher of the year award, he won a Christa McAuliffe award and a Newberry Foundation Fellowship. For Dennis, though, his greatest accomplishment has nothing to do with awards, fellowships, or even grants. "My greatest contribution and accomplishment in education," he says, "is my ability to motivate and instill in students the desire to learn and in the development of their self-esteem and self-confidence. I design my student study units with several common elements regardless of the content. . . . I design the unit to involve the entire class to work as a group with each individual responsible for specific elements of the project. Another element is in assuring that each individual is assigned a task that will challenge his/her ability. It will require the students to stretch beyond his/her learning comfort zone. Accountability to the group and to me are implicit in the design.

"The basic concept of my teaching," he explains succinctly, "is that I teach to individual students, not to a class." Dennis leans on Madeline Hunter's *Instructional Theory into Practice* when planning lessons. In this system, "students are provided detailed weekly lesson plans with the grading rubrics for major assignments included. During class I heavily rely on the Teacher Expectation and Student Achievement model of class discussion by blending questioning and redirection methodologies with the Bloom Taxonomy Model." He even gives each student a copy of the Bloom model to keep in their folders. He frequently talks to them about moving toward higher levels of learning and questioning.

These efforts don't go unnoticed. A colleague, Alice Rockhill, states that Dennis "provides alternative teaching modes for students who may be auditory, visual, or hands-on learners. With his kind support and encouragement, the question becomes when, not if, the student will learn the materials."

Dennis has several reasons for caring so deeply about his students' success, and several ways of contributing to their well-being and that of the community. One of his most popular contributions is a student-run TV station. "I designed, found funding for, and now operate the local community-access cable television station from my classroom. I post all community news concerning meetings and special events on the cable channel. I supervise my students as they design the pages for our twenty-four-hour-a-day broadcast. I also supervise my students in the production and broadcast to the community of all home volleyball games, basketball games, concerts, plays, and other school events."

In 1996 this TV station was called into action when the area was hit by a natural disaster. "During the flood, my students and I operated the cable television center, and my classroom became a command center for the Red Cross and emergency services." The experience provided an amazing example of a school giving back to its community. Dennis Griner isn't just an A+ educator and an A+ grant writer, he is an A+ human being. Perhaps someday financing will not be so scarce and that grant-writing talent won't be so necessary.

Compliments to the Teacher

Beverly Fox, superintendent of Palouse Schools, says, "Although Dennis is a humble person, he has a wealth of knowledge about teaching and working with children. If professional teacher cloning was possible, we would use him as the model!"

With Open Arms:
Nebraska's Mary Schlieder

A Defining Moment

"Every spring when I attend the graduation ceremony," Mary says, "I experience this 'definitive moment.' We have nearly a 100 percent graduation rate, even for the most troubled students." Despite being honored by the state of Nebraska, she says that the most important recognition "comes from proud parents and students who have overcome seemingly overwhelming odds and made it to graduation day."

Mary Schlieder began teaching back when special education was just an afterthought. Some schools had actual programs for their disabled students, while others just shipped them out to specialized schools. Worse still were those schools that simply came up with some sort of out-of-sight, out-of-mind solution. It is almost too painful to bear when one considers how many kids were neglected and how much potential was never tapped into.

Mary has seen the changes that came with the passing of the Individuals with Disabilities Education Act and the recent No Child Left Behind legislation. A teacher since 1980, she has run her own resource room since 1999. She also teaches two English classes and an independent study School-to-Career class for high-ability learners, as in most states Gifted and Talented students fall under the special education umbrella. For her ability to work with a wide range of students and for her willingness to meet their needs, in 2008 the state of Nebraska recognized Mary as its teacher of the year.

Lindsey Oelling, a student mentor in Mary's resource room at Norris High School in Firth, Nebraska, says, "I think she deserves the award because she cares about her students like her own kids. She treats them like they're not just someone she has to see every day."

Awards and compliments are nice, but for Mary, it's all about the kids. "I am rewarded when a student who previously had Fs shares his excitement with me as he shows his report card with all Cs and above. I am rewarded when a student who required tremendous academic help the year before can do nearly all of his work by himself. I feel a sense of satisfaction when no one would recognize that a particular girl has Asperger's syndrome and poor social skills because now she's sitting talking in the cafeteria with her Circle of Friends group." Circle of Friends is a peer-based approach to supporting kids with an autistic spectrum disorder and can be extremely beneficial for those struggling with social skills. Mary knows how important good grades are, but that friendships are even more important to kids.

"She inspires me," says Dylan, a student who has Asperger's syndrome. "She really pushes me to do it. She explains things piece by piece."

Mary says she approaches all of her students in this manner. "My philosophy is just don't give up. I just don't give up on anybody. Failure's not an option."

Mary knows that the same is true for teachers, but that it is hard to succeed if the teacher has not been adequately trained in differentiated instruction and classroom management. So she meets with them and contributes to their growth, which in turn contributes to the growth of their students. Listen to Mary's words and you know that she truly believes what she says. "I am rewarded when a group of colleagues volunteers to join me in a learning team reading a book to try to understand and better work with academically and behaviorally at-risk students. Teaching allows me to be an important part of so many lives, to touch a future I'll never see, to make a difference. I can't imagine any other career."

Mary cares so deeply about sharing her knowledge that she even published a book, *With Open Arms: Creating Supportive School Communities for Socially Challenged Kids Using Circle of Friends, Extracurricular Activities, and Staff Learning Teams*. Her goal when she wrote this book was to help teachers in their work with troubled students and to help parents work better with their struggling children. The book has become one of her teaching tools, whenever she is conducting or contributing to a professional development session. After working with her fellow teachers, Mary hopes they will go on to form learning teams that then discuss the latest research and collaborate to create an action plan. She says, "I speak to other school staff on the material in the book and have developed a Web site and do free conference calls for educators across the country. . . . I'm passionate about inclusion of students with behavioral and social difficulties and love to share methods that work with other staff who struggle with them."

For touching that future and for making that difference, the students of Norris High School are grateful. For taking what she knows about all different kinds of learners and helping her colleagues understand what it takes to teach them, she is an A+ educator.

Educational Philosophy

Mary's book, *With Open Arms*, provides parents and teachers with practical tools to help kids overcome social challenges. The book is supplemented by her Web site, www.schoolswithopenarms.com.

Policeman Turned Teacher Turned Dean: Florida's Samuel R. Bennett

In 2006 Samuel R. Bennett was a finalist for National Teacher of the Year. Before he could reach that rarified air, though, he had to be named Florida's teacher of the year, and that is no easy feat. He was chosen from more than 177,000 public school teachers. The criteria for Florida's teacher of the year are an outstanding ability to teach, knowledge of subject matter and the ability to communicate that knowledge, efforts at improving oneself while also contributing to the professional development of others, a well-defined philosophy of teaching, and an exceptional record of school and community service. On top of that, the teacher must demonstrate the skills needed to inspire a love of learning in students of all backgrounds and abilities. Samuel demonstrated all of the above and then some.

After being named teacher of the year, Samuel Bennett served as Florida's Christa McAuliffe Ambassador for Education. His responsibilities included touring the state to discuss the state of education and to focus on helping his fellow teachers raise student achievement. This is typical of many state teachers of the year, but Samuel's path to the fifth grade classroom at Garner Elementary School is different from that of all the other A+ educators. In the 1970s Samuel was a police officer in St. Petersburg, and that experience led him to the classroom. He said he wanted to get to the root of the problem, to help children *before* they ended up on the wrong side of the law. Dealing with them as a police officer, he felt that in too many cases it was just too late to point the person in the right direction. But as a teacher, perhaps he could make a difference.

Samuel earned his doctorate in organizational leadership from Nova Southeastern University and is now dean of its College of Education. This means Samuel has taught at just about every kind of educational institution, including elementary school and middle school, community college and in adult education. He serves on the boards of the Florida League of Christian Schools and the Florida Education Foundation and was president of the Winter Haven Optimist Club.

Mark Rutland, president of Southeastern University, says, "Dr. Bennett represents the very best in leadership and in classroom skills." So it is that nowadays Samuel helps future educators learn the intricacies of lesson planning and communicating with colleagues and parents, the legalities of special education, and the ins and outs of assessment. One class he teaches is Advanced Methods of Teaching Reading, and he has spent time researching such timely topics as parental involvement in education, educational learning communities, ethics, cooperative learning, and retaining good teachers. The most useful aspect of a good teacher prep program, though, is classroom management, and Samuel takes an approach that is becoming more and more common: creating bonds rather than acting as a disciplinarian. Building relations with students via this method also seems to work when trying to help a new teacher or even a veteran who has lost his or her spark. All teachers know a concept is more easily memorized when a mnemonic device is used and so, with that in mind, Samuel teaches about HEART. He advises, "Become a teacher with a heart: H—help others, E—encourage others, A—an attitude that is positive and contagious, R—reach out to the hurting and lonely, T—teach others/mentor others."

"I believe that I aim for the heart with my students," he says when asked what enabled him to stand apart from those 177,000 other teachers. "I help them feel better about themselves first, and then the learning can take place."

After walking the beat for so many years, Samuel is able to walk in shoes of those he teaches. Understanding "what it's like out there," he has even developed a program for single parents. The purpose is to help them cope with the stress of raising school-age children all by themselves. But when asked about his finest moment as a teacher, his thoughts return to the elementary school where he made a name for himself.

"I worked with a student—Steven from Haiti. He had behavioral and academic deficiencies. We continued to work on both areas and he became my 'Turnaround Student of the Year.' At the end of the year, Steven made this statement—'I wish you were my dad.' Steven was in my fifth-grade class. He is now in high school and I am still involved in his life. I want to see him succeed all the way through college."

Samuel is the kind of teacher who will go to great lengths to reach students like Steven. One of the things he was recognized for was his originality in the classroom. Rather than sticking with the same old gimmicks, he was comfortable thinking outside of the box. One example that provides a nice visual is that he would sometimes dress up as the character his students were reading about that day. His goal was to bring the material to life, to excite the kids about the story so he could teach them reading–comprehension skills. He certainly dresses the part of A+ educator!

In His Own Words

Although it was hard for Samuel to leave the classroom for the dean position at Southeastern University, he justified the move by saying, "I will be having an impact on many, many classrooms, rather than just one."

The Art of Teaching:
Idaho's Carol Scholz

——————— *A Defining Moment* ———————
Ask Carol about the teaching moment she enjoys most and her answer is no surprise. It's the enthusiasm of her response that leaves an impression, though. For her, these words are anything but clichéd. "My most important accomplishment is the 'Aha!' moment every child I teach experiences, as they master skills and discover the world!"

Some teachers have done it all. Idaho Arts Charter School's Carol Scholz is one of those teachers. Certified in both special education and elementary education, she has taught for more than twenty years. She has worked with students who are visually impaired and with those who are severely disabled. She has taught children with autism. She has taught first, second, third, and fourth grade, logging nine years with her second-graders before moving into her current position with third- and fourth-graders. In addition to all that teaching, Carol has received several technology and arts grants. Actually, thirteen grants in all. She has served as a mentor in a technology program for disabled students, and she has even taught an online class, teaching grant writing for Northwest Nazarene University. Chess, anyone? Carol can handle it. She has trained educators in the First Move program, a chess curriculum for elementary schools developed by the American Foundation for Chess. Chess is a useful extracurricular activity for those hoping to improve math skills. In particular, practice in number sense, spatial visualization, geometry, logic, and critical thinking are among the benefits, and that's why Idaho officially adopted it as a supplemental math curriculum. Carol got involved with the First Move program to help her students, but now she does so to help her fellow teachers. Recently, almost 150 teachers serving more than fifty thousand students gathered to learn the program she loves so much. Just as she supports the chess players at Idaho Arts, Carol has shown her love for the musicians. When she was named teacher of the year, Carol received $1,000—and gave the money away. "I decided to donate that back to the school for the band. They're in desperate need of instruments."

Carol's fifteen minutes of fame were not to be wasted. She immediately took the opportunity to talk about what she believes in. And then, with the theme of her magnet school in mind: "I want to take this opportunity to promote the arts in education. It really is in the forefront of research-based education. It's not just everyone just singing and dancing around. Project-based learning motivates them to be lifelong learners."

Some people question magnet schools and some question a school with an arts theme, especially in this age of high-stakes testing. Carol, though, sees the possibilities rather than the potential drawbacks. "I am now teaching at a school that allows me to fully integrate the arts into the curriculum, which research has shown leads to increased learning! We are in the business of creating the next generation of artists, scientists, and mathematicians as integrating the arts leads to academic achievement increases across the board."

Some teachers love their school so much that their name becomes synonymous with it, their pedagogy so completely in tune with its mission statement that their place there just seems a natural fit. Carol is a guiding light within the Idaho Arts Charter School and uses its theme to guide so much of what she does in the classroom. "She will volunteer for any committee that you need help on. She will try different teaching ideas. She is the most helpful, kind teacher," says her principal, Jackie Collins. State Superintendent of Public Instruction Tom Luna adds, "Scholz has served as an innovative leader in every school that she has worked in throughout her career. She goes above and beyond to mentor new teachers, develop curriculum, and readily share her expertise with others. Scholz exemplifies the quality and innovative teacher we need in every Idaho classroom."

If Carol hasn't done it all, she's come awfully close. Not only is she Idaho's top teacher, she survived the rigorous process of earning National Board Certification. With a spirit this creative and innovative, with the willpower to do it all, it's no wonder Carol Scholz is an A+ educator.

In Her Own Words

Carol is in favor of paying teachers, stating her support for a "program which will actually reward students and teachers across the board for performance. I think it is going to be so effective in not only raising achievement but encouraging people to do their best."

Taking the Voodoo Out of Economics:
Kentucky's Sherleen S. Sisney

A quarter of a century ago, Sherleen Sisney tried to warn America that "economic illiteracy" was a serious problem. This was in 1984, the year she was named National Teacher of the Year. One generation later, the United States is in deep debt, both its people and its government—if only Sherleen's words had been heeded. At the time of her award, just thirteen states required economics for their high school students.

When Sherleen was named the nation's best teacher, she was a teacher of economics, history, and political science at Louisville's Ballard High School. Just a few years earlier the Louisville public school system went bankrupt and had to merge with the Jefferson County schools. Needless to say, the district needed some good news. Sherleen was recognized for her work in the classroom as well as for the way she reached out for help. For example, with the help of the Junior League of Louisville, Sherleen started the Schools-Business Project, which brings local businesspeople into the classroom to lecture, answer questions, and conduct seminars and debates. The businessmen and businesswomen involved also arrange field trips, set up independent projects, and provide money or materials to teachers.

Within the classroom, Sherleen developed an economic system in which chips are used as the class currency. Each student earns these chips during class activities and can spend them during other class activities. "The lights are utilities, squares in the floor are commercial property, chairs are residential property. If they don't own a chair, they have to sit on the floor," Sherleen explains. "They may provide entertainment for the classes to earn more chips, or sell food." The more chips awarded, the stronger the economy. Businesses pop up to meet growing needs. This is what Sherleen wants to see in her classroom and in the country as a whole.

"The student's grade is based not on how successful he or she was in earning money or managing his or her financial empire, but on the diary that must be kept to trace and detail what they have done," she says. "Earning the greatest number of chips does not necessarily guarantee the best grade."

It is a system that really works. And back in 1984, it was a system, and a philosophy, appreciated by none other than the president.

"You know how it is with young children when they aren't loved," said President Ronald Reagan at the ceremony to honor Sherleen. "They think themselves unlovable, and that's the beginning of trouble. But when a teacher comes along and gives that child attention, shows him or her kindness, and makes them feel special, then for the first time, the child feels self-esteem and self-worth. And they blossom in the warmth. Your kindness and the values you live by echo down the decades, shaping the adults, the citizens they'll become."

Of course Sherleen cares deeply for her students, but she prefers to focus on the curriculum and how it will benefit her kids down the road. With the units she designs, Sherleen demonstrates what an important part of citizenship economic competency is. As she has moved from earning a master's degree at the University of Louisville to serving as the social studies department chair at Ballard, to directing the Governor's Scholars Program, she has kept in mind that most of her students are less than one year away from graduating high school and entering the "real world." This impending reality is especially important for her at-risk students, so she took on the responsibility of administering the Effective Learning Program (ELP) for them.

"I find that not all my students are similarly advantaged," says Sherleen. "Therefore, I talk in terms of what they can do." For her, economic competency is the great equalizer; economic illiteracy, a guarantee that the cycle of poverty will go on unbroken. She tells her students, "We are going to have to interact with our economic system, whether we want to or not. It is better to do it knowledgeably."

"If you expect the people to be ignorant and free, you expect what never was and never will be," President Reagan said at her ceremony, quoting Thomas Jefferson. This is obviously an opinion that Sherleen and the president have in common.

One useful tool in the fight against ignorance is teamwork. This is an important aspect of Sherleen's lessons and units, and she likes to expand the concept of team to the world outside her classroom. "When teachers can involve community resource people—including parents—in what they are trying to do with their students, and use these resources in a meaningful, educational way, I think the attention becomes natural, positive, and supportive." This serves to explain her dedication to the Schools-Business Project and to her efforts to keep parents informed of student progress so they can help at home.

Sherleen knows that caregiver involvement is important but that there is only so much a teacher can do to encourage it. Therefore, she has spent time developing her ideas on helping new teachers. She understands that the greatest guarantee of success for the students is having qualified, well-trained teachers. "I would definitely recommend more practicum, more experiences in actual teaching, than a student teacher can gain in nine to twelve weeks of student teaching. Prospective teachers need guidance during their student teaching and we need to develop ways to have quality control in a situation where student teachers are growing and learning."

Back in the days of Reaganomics, also known as "voodoo economics," Sherleen Sisney was a teacher ahead of her time. She understood the importance of an informed populace and what was at risk if our schools continued to graduate students unprepared to handle the economic responsibilities of adulthood. Only an A+ educator could have such prescience. Only an A+ educator could continue to fight the good fight in the face of trickle-down economics and all too many states failing to allow the teaching of economics to trickle down to students.

In Her Own Words

Economics is the most relevant aspect of any curriculum I've ever been involved with. . . . It's going to have an impact on the whole lives of students.

Closure

Across America today, there are teachers of varying quality, and the difference is due to a number of circumstances and personal decisions. No one can say for sure why one teacher is an A+ educator or why another teacher is of such a poor quality that he or she is "failing." It is easy to point out the traits that lead to the grade, but it isn't so easy to answer the question why.

Some teachers are exhausted after many years in the field. Others are exhausted after just a couple of months and are scanning the Internet for other opportunities or other career paths. Some teachers entered the classroom for the wrong reason and will hopefully exit the classroom for the right reason. Some teachers have such high expectations of themselves that to be anything less than a great teacher would be the equivalent of swallowing thumb tacks. Some teachers have a voice in their head that reminds them of a child they once knew and drives them to create a better future for the children they now know. Whether a teacher is a B- educator or a D+ educator or just your average, run-of-the-mill C teacher, they all have something to learn from the A+ educators. If you are one of these struggling teachers and you took the time to read about all of these high-achieving teachers, then your heart is in the right place. You care enough to push yourself in your chosen profession. You gave your free time to read about best practice and what has worked for others, and that means you want to be the best teacher you can be.

Just as teachers implore their students to try harder or maybe to simply try something different, the same advice applies to teachers. Even these A+ educators try new things every now and again. Innovation and the search for better methods is a boon in all fields, but especially in education. In areas where children can't search for themselves, can't advocate for themselves, and can't provide for themselves the lessons that will help them grow, it is the teacher's job to do so. And every time a failing teacher gets his or her grade up, the students benefit. The hope is that once enough teachers get their personal grades up, they will no longer be failing, their schools will no longer be failing, and the students will no longer be failing. All of this will snowball, gaining momentum as success builds upon success, until finally the day no one ever thought would arrive comes to America's schools as the nation's children give us an A+ and the world begins once more to look upon our education system as a model of success.

08/18/10